GIFT AND RESPONSE

A Biblical Spirituality
for
Contemporary Christians

Carolyn Thomas

Paulist Press

New York/Mahwah

Library of Congress Cataloging-in-Publication Data

Thomas, Carolyn,   1936-
    Gift and response : a biblical spirituality for contem-
porary Christians / Carolyn Thomas.
        p.   cm.
    Includes bibliographical references.
    ISBN 0-8091-3510-8 (pbk.)
    1. Spiritual life—Catholic Church.   2. Catholic Church
—Doctrines.   I. Title.
BX2350.2.T495   1994   94-32835
242—dc20   CIP

Published by Paulist Press
997 Macarthur Boulevard
Mahwah, New Jersey 07430

Printed and bound in the
United States of America

To my sisters and brothers:

Jane and Bernadette
Joe and Patsy; George and Pat; Jim and Luisa;
Julian and Maureen;
Glen and Doris

CONTENTS

PREFACE

In my first book, *Will the Real God Please Stand Up*, I wrote about the authentic biblical God who is loving, forgiving, caring and consoling. I demonstrated through the use of scripture that our God calls us to personal growth, away from the unauthentic images of an angry, vindictive and intolerant God. Many people harbor these false images because of distorted religious education or unfortunate life experiences.

The One who consistently gifts us with love, even if we do not love in return, patiently awaits our response. My desire to respond to God's fidelity by living faithfully and gratefully in our world has been primarily inspired by my study of sacred scripture, and by the goals and objectives of my congregation, the Sisters of Charity of Nazareth. Biblical reflections convinced me that to live in God's image and likeness is to live in responsible relationship to all of God's creation and to make visible the creative presence of our loving God in daily life. My desire to allow people and the ordinary aspects of life to become a vital part of my relationship with God sparked my interest in writing this book. Life is God's gift; the opportunities we encounter in life challenge our response.

At the end of each chapter, I have listed some biblical passages, "*For Further Reflection.*" My hope is that the reader will first read the chapter meditatively and then spend some time in reflection on the passages cited. In that way, the book will more effectively aid the reader in deepening his or her relationship with God and all of creation.

In addition to the scripture readings for reflection, I have supplied a limited bibliography of "*Suggested Readings*" at the end of each chapter. The bibliography is not totally restricted to biblical resource books for two reasons. First, biblical resources dealing with the topics I treated in some of the chapters are scarce. Second, I believe that once the reader has the biblical background from the chapter, he or she can read non-biblically based books from a biblical perspective.

I wish to acknowledge the persons who helped in various ways to bring this book to fruition: Mary Ransom Burke, S.C.N., Kathy Gaiser and Marie Mudd who so graciously read my manuscript and made suggestions for revisions; Peter Veraka and Beverly Lane, librarians at the Pontifical College Josephinum, whose assistance was invaluable; Mary Pat Mulligan and my other colleagues, friends, and students at the Josephinum whose encouragement and help enabled the book to be completed; my nephew, Dale Thomas, and my nieces, Barbara Thomas and Pat Tomaszewski for their insights and contributions; my family and other friends, especially Mary and Jim Anderson; Sisters Jean Frances Thomas, Albert Louise Thompson, Janice Downs, and all the Sisters of Charity of Nazareth who kept asking for my next book, and whose lives have taught me much about what I have written.

FOREWORD

Seeing how the events of life all fit together will certainly be one of the joys of eternity. We will probably realize, first of all, how the many bits and pieces of our individual lives became the precious threads of a well-woven tapestry. Then, as our vision widens, God may let us see how various events of world history influenced, not only other events, but also the thinking of whole generations. Some of these things we know already, but is it not possible that what we now know will become clearer in eternity?

Meanwhile, scholars of many disciplines help us even today to gain some new insights for which their gifts and their persevering use of those gifts have cleared the way. *Gift and Response*, by scripture scholar Carolyn Thomas offers opportunities for such insights, some of which touch the heart and even—if we allow them—move us to action.

Mountains and valleys, streams and waterfalls, clouds, stars, wind, rain and all the other gifts of creation have inspired prayer and poetry since the beginning of time. The first chapter of this book invites the reader to enter fully into the experience of the present moment so as to allow nature to serve as a medium of God's fidelity and love. Entering into this experience today, however, means encountering nature in the bold light of what science is telling us about the future of the environment. Nature is still a medium of God's fidelity. The faithfulness of our response is being challenged.

To love one's neighbor as oneself has always been a goal of every true Christian. To pursue that goal in today's society means being a conscientious citizen, we are told in the second chapter. We are not left in doubt as to what citizenship really means.

For people who have always had a home and who have no fear of losing that home, it is difficult to imagine being homeless. Chapter 3 of *Gift and Response* reminds us that we have not here on earth a lasting homeland. We are homeless, a people on a journey toward our true home, having much in common with our sisters and brothers who are living on the streets and under bridges.

Chapter 4 indicates that Jesus was an alien and, in light of that view, focuses on aliens in our country and in many other countries today. We see how a biblical spirituality embraces the alien, uniting that person's pain to the pain of the God who became human and was rejected by the people.

Chapter 5 takes up the role of women in the church, showing how the church of today is being deprived of the gifts of women just at a time when those gifts are greatly needed. This chapter reviews Jesus' dealings with women in the gospels. It examines women's role in the Pauline church and the reasons for the decreased role in the post-Pauline period.

Many people today have difficulty with the process of aging, in themselves and in others. Growing older, with the emphasis on *growing*, is the subject of chapter 6 of this book. It characterizes the time of growing old as a time of grace and of intensified relationship with God and with other people.

Has there ever been a time when the subject of physical fitness was more prominent than it is today? Chapter 7 emphasizes the importance of our bodies as integral to worship, communication, sensual delight, and service to other people. Physical fitness, therefore, is advocated as a preparation for carrying out our baptismal commitment and for authentic living in the image and likeness of God.

Faithfulness in a variety of relationships has been acclaimed throughout history and literature. Today, however, statistics on unfaithfulness and its acceptance as inevitable are frightening. In chapter 8 we encounter through scripture a faithful God whose fidelity is the basis of all relationships.

On this note of God's faithfulness, Sister Carolyn brings to a close a series of rich reflections on scripture that are particularly appropriate for the end of an era. They are equally appropriate for integration into one's spirituality in an era soon to begin.

Mary Ransom Burke, S.C.N.

1

Harmony with Nature

O God, how multifold are your works!
In wisdom you have made them all,
*the earth is full of your creatures (Ps 104:24).**

The people of the Bible walked amidst the silence of Palestine's desert sands. They knew the relief of a gentle breeze and of a friendly oasis where water meant the difference between life and death. They pastured sheep on the quiet and lonely slopes of Judea's mountains and foothills. They were a people familiar with the lush green valleys and highlands of Galilee. They knew well the experience of cool water that refreshed tired feet, quenched thirst, and moistened parched lips. Biblical people knew the song of birds and the fragrance of flowers, the majesty of mountains and the freshness of streams, the habits of animals, the smell of soil and the whisper of wind—all these were part of their experiential universe.

Not surprisingly, therefore, the world of nature plays a major role in biblical spirituality. God's people in the Old Testament, as well the people of the New Testament, were keenly aware of the beauty and goodness of nature. Their awareness was not dulled by the constant noise of fast-moving locomotion, nor was their attention diverted by ringing phones, blaring radios and flashing TV. Theirs was a world of quietude interwoven only by human interaction and nature's communication.

Engaging the Present

A biblical spirituality that embraces the world's environment begins with a keen awareness of God's gifts in

---

* All scripture quotations are taken from the NRSV, unless otherwise noted.

the world. Basic to such awareness is a reverence and appreciation for the present moment. If we are always rushing from one activity to another, all the while planning the future, we live in the "not yet," the unpredictable. The present, however, is our only certainty; the future may never come. If we live in an imaginary future, the present with all its gifts and surprises may easily be sacrificed to the god of frenzy.

Only by living the present moment are we capable of using all our senses to respond to the world around us. Awareness of that which we see at the present—what we hear, smell, feel, and taste—enables us to make the present moment a prayer. Many of the psalms are poetic prayers of persons who lived in the grace of the present moment and who were fully aware of the world of nature. Psalm 65 comprises reflections of a person who thought creatively about God as one who works with all aspects of nature. In this one psalm alone, God is portrayed in relation to the earth as a civil engineer, a landscaper, a musician, a farmer, a parent clothing its offspring:

> You set the mountains in place by your power...
> You still the roaring of the seas....
> The farthest east and west you make resound with
>   joy.
> You have visited the land and watered it...
> You have prepared the land....
>
> The fields are garmented with flocks
> and the valleys are blanketed with grain.
> They shout and sing for joy (Ps 65:7–14; NAB).

An awareness of the experiences which the present moment affords has the potential to fill our hearts with gratitude to God for the things we encounter and from which we draw life. Sensitivity coupled with gratitude engenders reverence for the earth and its benefits.

Century after century, our planet has gifted us with life, sustenance and pleasure, so that our days are punctuated with reminders of God's loving presence and care for us. From season to season, with panorama after panorama, unique gifts are unfolded before us. The sun plays hide and seek in and out of silky clouds that wind their way across a blue-domed sky. Trees harbor fledglings as they stretch their necks for new worms and chirp their first song. Soft, furry creatures dart in and out of nature's camouflage. White-capped mountains keep silent vigil as rustling streams give birth to rivers that course their paths into mighty oceans. The hush of winter snow gives way to green hills patched with wild flowers.

The splendor of nature has inspired song, dance, drama, art, literature, meditation, and prayer. In Psalm 109, the psalmist, using poetic simile, pours out his plight to God:

> I am gone like a shadow at evening
> I am shaken off like a locust (Ps 109:23; RSV).

The deer provided the inspiration for Psalm 42:

> As a deer longs for running water,
> So my soul thirsts for you, my God. (Ps 42:1; NJB)

Charles Cummings in his *Eco-Spirituality* rightly identifies the Irish poet, Joseph Mary Plunkett, as one whom nature incited to poetic prayer:

I See His Blood Upon the Rose

> I see His blood upon the rose
>   And in the stars the glory of His eyes,
> His body gleams amid eternal snows,
>   His tears fall from the skies.
> I see His face in every flower;
>   The thunder and the singing of the birds
> Are but His voice—and carven by His power
>   Rocks are His written words.
> All pathways by His feet are worn,
>   His strong heart stirs the ever-beating sea,

His crown of thorns is twined with every thorn,
    His cross is every tree.[1]

More and more people are realizing not only the practical value of preserving our environment, but also its aesthetic and ascetic importance. Considerable progress in environmental concerns has been made in the last few years. For example, the year 1990 marked the birth of Earth Day, a worldwide effort to turn the tide of global devastation. An estimated 200 million people from 140 countries participated in activities to save the earth and to make people more aware of impending disaster should the pattern of human disregard continue unabated. The events that occurred gave rise to subsequent years of growth in an emphasis on caring for the earth.[2]

A spirituality which reflects appreciation and concern for the preservation of the environment makes possible the reversal of the tide of planetary destruction. Our religious heritage utilizes and validates a spirituality that includes efforts to make the earth a safe place for us and our descendants.

Trusted Sojourners

Our religious tradition offers us a challenge to care for the environment. Sadly, however, misinterpretation of the first story of creation in Genesis has also been the cause for blaming our biblical tradition for much of the exploitation and diminution of life on the planet. The following quotation illustrates the point:

The earth was a creation of a monotheistic God, who, after shaping it, ordered its inhabitants, in the words of *Genesis*: "Be fruitful and multiply, and replenish the earth and subdue it: and have dominion over the fish of the sea and over the fowl of the air and over every living thing that moveth upon the earth." Thus the spread of Christianity, which is generally considered to have paved the way for the development of technology, may at the same time have carried the seeds of the wanton exploitation of nature that often accompanied technical progress.[3]

These allegations do not reflect a true picture of our creator God as portrayed in the first chapter of Genesis. As is the case of all scripture, isolated passages have to be understood in the context of the whole. Genesis 1 presents our God in the semblance of an expectant parent getting ready for the birth of a child. The account is not a scientific one, meant to delineate the process of creation, but rather a theological account of God's love and wisdom in the creation of humanity and the world. God does not simply create human beings and drop them in the midst of chaos. No, our God carefully prepares a world for them from a "formless wasteland" (in Hebrew, *tohu wa-bohu*) and darkness. Even the sound of the Hebrew words seems to suggest disorder and aimlessness, emptiness and a lack of productivity.[4] God's concern is to prepare a world in which human beings can be happy and lead good and productive lives. After each creative act, the ingenious writer voices divine approval, "And God saw how good it was."

The climax of these creative acts was the creation of the woman and man in the image and likeness of God. They were given authority over the earth and dominion over wildlife. To live in the image and likeness of God is to imitate the creator. God brought order out of chaos, and as people made to God's image and likeness, we are to do likewise. To have dominion over other creatures is not to exploit, but to have dominion in the manner modeled by God. Creation was God's gift to us; we in turn are to gift future generations with a fruitful and safe earth. Our privilege as images of God is to live in responsible relationship with all of creation.[5]

In the Old Testament, the land is said to belong to

God (Josh 22:19), and the people to whom it was entrusted were to cultivate it and enjoy its fruits (Dt 26:1–11). The earth has been consigned to our stewardship, and it needs our care, our wise and judicious use of its natural resources. God's word in sacred scripture provides us with an ideal. The book of Exodus tells the story of the Hebrews wandering in the desert after their release from slavery in Egypt. As illustrated in this narrative, God never sanctioned greed even among those who previously suffered tremendous want. Each day manna rained down from heaven for them to eat:

> The one that gathered much had nothing over, and the one that gathered little had no lack; each gathered according to what was needed to eat (Ex 16:18; based on RSV).

Learn from the Sparrows

By portioning out the manna day by day, God was teaching the people to live in a spirit of simplicity. Later, this simple life-style was abandoned by King Solomon whose greed and extravagance violated the ideal set forth by God. The Old Testament writer of 1 Kings ties the abuse of human beings to greed and misuse of natural resources. In a matter-of-fact way, he mentions that Adoniram "was in charge of forced labor" (1 Kgs 4:6) which numbered thirty thousand men out of all Israel (1 Kgs 5:13); that Solomon "had twelve officers over all Israel, who provided food for the king and his household" (1 Kgs 4:7), and that "they let nothing be lacking"; that provisions for the king's household "for one day was thirty cors of fine flour, and sixty cors of meal, ten fat oxen, and twenty pasture-fed cattle, a hundred sheep, besides harts, gazelles, roebucks and fatted fowl" (1 Kgs 4:22-23). The temple Solomon built for God took only seven years to build (1 Kgs 6:38), whereas the completion of Solomon's own house (1 Kgs 7:1) required thirteen years. Cedars from Lebanon were imported and used extravagantly (1 Kgs 5:6, 10) in these buildings as well as in the House of the Forest of Lebanon, the Hall of Pillars, the Hall of the Throne, the Hall of Judgment, and the house Solomon made for Pharaoh's daughter whom he had married (1 Kgs 7:2-8).

The first book of Kings (chapters 7 and 10) conveys the impression that other natural resources as well were used in excess—bronze, gold, costly stones, ivory and wild animals. Whatever Solomon wanted, he obtained regardless of its cost both in terms of human dignity and environmental abuse. Undoubtedly such exaggerations were meant to impress the reader with the waste that resulted from the king's greed and the burden it put upon the people of his land. Consequently, upon Solomon's death, the northern part of his kingdom rebelled against his oppression and set up its own king (1 Kgs 12). This event marked the division of the kingdom of Israel and the beginning of war between those living in the north and those in the south.

There is a clear connection in our ancient biblical tradition between lack of respect for human beings and degeneration of the land. When the people are no longer kind and faithful to one another and to God, nature itself is also affected. The prophet Hosea laments:

> Therefore the land mourns,
>   and all who dwell in it languish,
> and also the beasts of the field,
>   and the birds of the air;
>   and even the fish of the sea
>   are taken away (Hos 4:3; RSV).

Isaiah likewise links human sin with the earth's illnesses:

> The earth mourns and withers,
>   the world languishes and withers;
>   the heavens languish together with the earth.

The earth lies polluted
   under its inhabitants;
   for they have transgressed the laws,
      violated the statutes,
      broken the everlasting covenant (Is 24:5–6).

More than a century ago, Aldous Huxley (1864–1963) warned of a chain reaction within the universe when there is lack of respect for any part of creation:

> We begin by lacking charity towards Nature,...we try to dominate and exploit, we waste the earth's mineral resources, ruin its soil, ravage its forests, pour filth into its rivers and poisonous fumes into its air. From lovelessness in relation to Nature we advance to lovelessness in relation to art—a lovelessness so extreme that we have effectively killed all the fundamental or useful arts and set up various kinds of mass production by machines in their place. And of course this lovelessness in regard to art is at the same time a lovelessness in regard to the human beings who have to perform the fool-proof and grace-proof tasks imposed by our mechanical art-surrogates and by the interminable paperwork connected with mass-production and mass-distribution.[6]

A Time for Embracing

Paul's letter to the Romans challenges every Christian to care for the earth and for one another, and to nurture our relationships with Christ, human beings, and the earth. These ties find their basis in our union with Christ, a reality which Paul skillfully unfolds in chapter 8. He begins with our relationship with Christ and one another which bonds us with God. From there, Paul moves on to our solidarity with all of creation. His argument develops as follows. In baptism, we are united in a close bond with

Christ (Rom 6:6) which in turn makes us his brothers and sisters. That familial relationship to Christ enables us to call God "Abba" (Rom 8:15-6). Since we are co-heirs with Christ and since all that is God's belongs to Christ, then all that is Christ's becomes our heritage, "provided we suffer with him in order that we may be glorified with him" (Rom 8:17; RSV).

Paul then moves to the source of our suffering. Those who belong to the Spirit and those who belong to the flesh belong to opposing forces. Those who are committed to the Spirit of Christ have their minds devoted to the things of the Spirit which bring life and peace. Those opposed to the way of Christ's Spirit among us belong to the flesh; they are hostile to God and hence face death (Rom 8:5-8). Paul identifies these hostile forces in Romans 1 as self-idolaters, as people who are turned in upon themselves so as to make self the criterion of all values.

Two such opposing forces are bound to clash and result in suffering for sincere and committed Christians. With the Spirit as their leader, however, they will be able to enter enemy territory created by the realm of the flesh. The suffering that ensues is a suffering with Christ which in turn will lead to glory with him (Rom 8:17-18).

Paul points out that we are not only in close union with Christ and other people, but we are also in solidarity with all of creation. Human beings, together with non-human creation, groan in expectation of deliverance from corruption (Rom 8:19-21). Paul does not think of the final coming of Christ in glory in terms of the destruction of the world as does the author of the book of Revelation. Rather, Paul speaks in terms of everything created as groaning and waiting to achieve the purpose of its creation: "Creation itself will be set free from its bondage to decay and obtain the glorious liberty of the children of God" (Rom 8:21; RSV).

Our Judeo-Christian tradition then provides not only an ideal but a challenge as well. The bond of human beings with all of creation which was initiated by God from the beginning of time is ours to nourish or to sever. The former choice has the potential to develop into a more intimate relationship with God, a relationship that is constantly nurtured by all of creation. The latter choice can only produce unnecessary human suffering and deprivation, because human beings share with the environment its fate or its fortune.

Sowing Our Future

Scientists warn us that our planet is ill, that we are not in rhythm with its giving and needing to receive. As Christians face the dilemma of an ailing planet, we "hope for what we do not see" (Rom 8:25), because our faith assures us that the resurrection of Christ from the dead makes all things possible (Rom 8:35-39). Even a mere spark of hope can be kindled to a flame of action if our lives are firmly rooted in God's word in the scriptures. Awareness of the present moment's gifts from and in nature is a first step in walking unflinchingly to meet our challenge with the Spirit leading us (Rom 8:4).

Environmentalists are helpful in alerting us to areas of concern. The question, "What can I do?" is frequently discouraging, because one person cannot resolve problems that world leaders have been unable or unwilling to solve.

Christians need not be intimidated by seemingly impossible tasks. The feeling of helplessness that tempts us to inactivity when we are faced with gigantic local and global problems can be converted into Spirit-filled creativity. Strengthened and led by the Spirit of Christ, we will find ways to hammer away at each task as it presents itself. In that mode of living, we will discover the means to transform into life-giving sources such sights as mountainous garbage dumps that presently reek with the odor of decay.

A spirituality that embraces and is nourished by creation takes seriously the notion of a simple life-style. Once we have taken stock of our own personal life-styles, we can move within our households, and from there to our neighborhoods, churches, cities and other organized groups.

Grassroots mobilization has proven effective in bringing about change in many difficult situations around the globe. In the United States, every person of age has the power to vote. Elected officials obtain their positions by proposing a platform of action which is based on what they perceive as important issues to their constituents. If ecology is a priority for ordinary citizens, it will become a priority for our legislators. Once legislators are convinced that the office they hold depends upon their influence to bring about change, action is bound to follow. Church, neighborhood, and city organizations can mobilize efforts to educate the public to the urgent task before us. Once the public is aware, ecological concerns can become strategic issues for election campaigns.

One ecologist has summarized his case well:

> The time has come—indeed it may be slipping away—for grassroots mobilization worldwide to put our civilization on a sustainable base. Until governments and international institutions join the struggle, it cannot succeed, but in the meantime hope lies with individual citizens. Our most gifted, young and old, have a critical role to play in the communities where they live. To be seeds of change, these men and women will need a clear personal vision and deep determination mixed with patience, humility, pragmatism, and insight.[7]

Praying with Nature

Not only do we need nature for practical reasons, but we also need it for our spiritual growth. One has only to walk outside after a time of isolation within the boundaries of brick and mortar to realize the power of nature to revive a person both physically and spiritually. The grandeur of a simple wildflower, the magnificence of a sunset, the sound of a breeze rustling fall leaves— every facet of nature has the potential to raise our hearts to God. Throughout the Bible, nature plays an important role in the expression of God's word to us:

> Praise Yahweh, sun and moon,
>   Praise Yahweh, all you shining stars!
> Praise Yahweh, you highest heavens,
>   and you waters above the heavens! (Ps 148:3–4; based on RSV)

In speaking of Judah's return from exile, the prophet Isaiah finds in the desert symbols of joy:

> The wilderness and the dry land
>   shall be glad,
> the desert shall rejoice
>   and blossom;
> like the crocus,
>   it shall blossom abundantly,
> and rejoice with joy and singing (Is 35:1; RSV).

When God responds to Job out of the whirlwind, the wondrous mysteries of nature serve as a basis for God's humorous self-defense:

> Do you know when the
>   mountain goats bring forth?
> Do you observe
>   the calving of the hinds?
> Do you give the horse
>   his might?
> Do you clothe his neck
>   with strength?
> Do you make him leap
>   like the locust?

His majestic snorting
  is terrible (Job 39:1, 19–20; RSV).

The gospels tell us that Jesus often walked by the Sea of Galilee. The mountains and desert also provided solitude for him when he wanted to get away and pray. His awareness of nature is reflected in his use of creation to explain our relationship to God or to emphasize a point which he wished to make. For example:

Foxes have holes,
and birds of the air have nests;
but the Son of man
has nowhere to lay his head (Lk 9:58; RSV).

Are not five sparrows sold for two pennies?
And not one of them is forgotten before God.
Why, even the hairs of you head are all
numbered. Fear not; you are of more value than
  many sparrows (Lk 12:6–7; RSV).

Living the Seasons

Living in rhythm with the seasons, especially in the northern hemisphere, is a means of nourishing our spirituality and sharpening our appreciation of nature and its gifts. The mood of each liturgical season coincides with the flow of the natural seasons of the year.

Springtime's burst of fresh growth and sunshine speak of new life and resurrection. The signs of new life can help us to reflect on the meaning of the reign of God in our daily lives and to be grateful for God's great gift in Jesus.

The season of summer, with its full-blown flowers and fresh vegetables, speaks of life lived to its fullness. In the summertime, especially, nature might inspire us to examine the extent to which we live life fully. For the Christian, life lived fully is the life of a faithful disciple. Jesus summarized the meaning of discipleship:

> If any want to become my followers, let them
> deny themselves and take up their cross and fol-
> low me. For those who want to save their life
> will lose it, and those who lose their life for my
> sake, and for the sake of the gospel, will save it
> (Mk 8:34–35).

To deny oneself is to break away from all self-centered-
ness which inhibits our following the risen Jesus. A person who is centered on self will not take the risks that
discipleship requires. The process of turning from self to
Christ and other people involves the cross; thus it is that
one loses one's life for the sake of Christ. Paradoxically,
that loss is the actual saving of our lives, for only in a life
of authentic discipleship will we experience the real
meaning of life, a life that bears abundant fruit in the
reign of God.

Autumn ushers in the harvest. All around us there
are signs of diminishment: fruits let go of their branches,
and vegetables their vines; the sun's rays are less direct;
green leaves take on burnished colors and flutter to the
ground; birds seek warmer climates; a general feeling of
melancholy fills the air. These signs of fall provide an
opportunity for us to take stock of our lives. This time of
the year invites us to look back with gratitude and to
ponder how God's grace has been at work in our lives
and to marvel at the fruit it has borne. Autumn is indeed
a time of thanks-giving.

Autumn also offers us a challenge to look forward
with an openness to whatever God still wishes to do in
us and through us. It may be, for example, that God is
asking us to let go of grudges, to forgive as we have been
forgiven. Forgiveness is an unmistakable mark of one
who claims to be a follower of Jesus:

> Love your enemies, do good to those who hate
> you, bless those who curse you, pray for those
> who abuse you.... If you love those who love you,

what credit is that to you? For even sinners do
the same.... Love your enemies, do good, and
lend, expecting nothing in return.... Be merciful,
just as your Father is merciful (Lk 6:27-36).

The norm of forgiveness that Jesus sets for his disciples is
the standard of God's own forgiveness; God forgives us
when we do not deserve forgiveness. Refusal to forgive
another is the only obstacle to God's forgiveness of us.

The winter season brings signs of death. Many trees
give the appearance of being dead; their limbs are bare
with no sign of life. Wild grass and flowers seem to die as
well. The signs of winter inspire us to reflect on death.
Death in itself is not good; that is why Jesus is said to
have "shuddered, moved from within with anger" when
he came to the tomb of Lazarus (Jn 11:38). Death was a
sign that Satan's rule had not been broken. But in raising
Lazarus, Jesus anticipated his resurrection which would
annul death and break Satan's reign.

Reflections on death need not be morose for a follower of Jesus. Like the trees and grass that will come to
life with the dawning of spring, so also will the disciple
experience new life following the death of the mortal
body. In John's gospel, Jesus tells his disciples that he
wants them to be with him where he is (Jn 17:24). He also
promised them:

If I go and prepare a place for you, I will come
again and will take you to myself, so that where
I am, there you may be also (Jn 14:3).

Nature, therefore, is one of our most ancient inspirations
for communion with God. One cannot imagine what it
would be like to read scripture without a personal experience of nature. If we let the earth speak its message to us,
God's love will be proclaimed every time we feast our eyes
upon it.

Summary

In our Judeo-Christian tradition, care and concern for creation is a divine commission which finds its roots in scripture. In Genesis, humanity is charged with stewardship of the earth and its gifts. The writings of Paul to the early Christian communities emphasize our solidarity with all of creation, human and non-human. Hence, Christian engagement and responsible relationship to both is part and parcel of our life in Christ.

Care for the earth has practical consequences for our spiritual life. Nature furnishes us with images of inspiration for our faith journey. The many facets of creation provide channels for God's love for us; their grandeur affords us an abundance of meaning inherent in our religious tradition. The seasons provide a natural flow for our relationship with God. Awareness of nature makes the psalms and Jesus' teaching come alive. As the following chapter demonstrates, a life of committed citizenship enhances our ability to live faithfully in relationship to all of creation.

For Further Reflection:

Job 38 and 39
Ps 95
Ps 148

Suggested Readings

Austin, Richard Cartwright. *Hope for the Land. Environmental Theology.* John Knox, 1988.

Bailey, Lloyd R. *Genesis, Creation, and Creationism.* Paulist, 1993.

Berry, C.P., Thomas with Thomas Clark, S.J. *Befriending the Earth. A Theology of Reconciliation between Humans and the Earth.* Holy Cross Center for Ecology and Spirituality, 1991.

Briere, Elizabeth. "Creation, Incarnation and Transfiguration," *Sobernost* 11-12 (1989-1990) 31-40.

Brueggemann, Walter. "Land: Fertility and Justice," *Interpretation and Obedience.* Fortress, 1991.

Bruteau, Beatrice. "Eucharistic Ecology and Ecological Spirituality." *Cross Currents* 40 (Winter, 1990-91) 499-514.

Bryne, S.J. Brendan. *Inheriting the Earth. A Pauline Basis for a Spirituality for Our Time.* Alba House, 1990.

Carpenter, Betsy. "The Whole Earth Agenda," *U.S. World Report* (Dec 25, 1989-Jan 1, 1990) 50-52.

Cummings, Charles. *Eco-Spirituality. Toward a Reverent Life.* Paulist, 1991.

"Companions in Creation" (The Florida Bishops' Pastoral Letter on the Environment). January 1, 1991. Reprinted in *Origins* 20 (February 1, 1991).

Christiansen, S.J., Drew. "Christian Theology and Ecological Responsibility," *America* 166:18 (May 23, 1992) 448-451.

Fitzgerald, William J. *Seasons of the Earth and Heart. Becoming Aware of Nature, Self, and Spirit.* Ave Maria, 1991.

Flynn, Eileen P. *Cradled in Human Hands.* Sheed and Ward, 1991.

French, William C. "Ecological Dangers and Christian Responsibility," *New Theology Digest* 4 (May, 1991) 26-42.

Fritch, Al. *Eco-Church: An Action Manual.* Resource Publications, 1992.

Graham, S.J., Robert Andrew, "The Environment and the Gospel," *Columbia* 70:22 (June, 1990) 22.

Hall, Douglas. *Imaging God.* Eerdmans, 1986.

Haught, John F. *The Promise of Nature.* Paulist, 1993.

Heidtke, John. *Getting Down to Earth: A Call to Environmental Action.* Paulist, 1993.

Johnson, Elizabeth A. *Women, Earth, and Creator Spirit.* Paulist, 1993.

Jung, Shannon. *We Are Home. A Spirituality of the Environment.* Paulist, 1993.

Lambrecht, Jan. "The Groaning Creation: a Study of Rom 8:18-30," *Louvain Studies* 15 (Spring, 1990).

Murray, Robert. *The Cosmic Covenant: Biblical Themes of Justice, Peace and the Integrity of Creation.* Sheed & Ward, 1992.

Nowell, Irene. "My Light, My Rock: Images of God in Nature," *The Bible Today* (March, 1991) 69-74.

2

Citizen and Sojourner

Truly I tell you,
just as you did it to the least of these...
you did it to me (Mt 25:40).

Luisa now spoke English, and she had worked hard to master its pronunciation. She had devoted herself faithfully to studying the United States Bill of Rights, and she could respond to any question about it without hesitation. She knew American history better than most native-born citizens. Finally, the day came. "I pledge allegiance to the flag...." Another happy person became a citizen of our country. "I'm going be a good citizen," my sister-in-law declared with moistened eyes. "My country will never be sorry that it granted me citizenship." Afterwards, we all went our separate ways, probably each of us continuing to take our own citizenship for granted. But Luisa didn't take anything for granted; she registered to vote and became involved in organizations that could make a difference in the lives of other people. She understood clearly the meaning of citizenship.

Servant of Two Worlds

This happy occasion of naturalization reminded me of something that Paul said in his letter to the Philippians: "Our citizenship is in heaven" (Phil 3:20). There is a big difference between obtaining naturalization in a country in this world and becoming a citizen of heaven. A person has to earn earthly citizenship by meeting specific requirements, such as language, knowledge of a citizen's rights, and familiarity with the country's history. No one, however, can earn citizenship in heaven. St. Paul states that when we were still weak and helpless, God gratuitously chose us for eternal life through the death of Jesus Christ. God made us citizens of heaven (Rom 5:6–8). Our heavenly citizenship, then, is God's gift to us, unearned and freely given out of love.

With the gift of citizenship in heaven, which occurs at baptism, God initiates an intimate union with us. We are "united" with Christ, Paul asserts (Rom 6:5). The word "united" in Greek, *symphytoi*, means to grow together as a grafted branch grows onto a tree. Just as the branch begins to share the life of the tree, so also do we begin to share God's life at baptism. As citizens of heaven, we also have the privilege of relating intimately to God as "Abba" (Rom 8:15). This family relationship makes us "heirs of God and joint heirs with Christ—if, in fact, we suffer with him so that we may be glorified with him" (Rom 8:17).

The privileges of earthly citizenship are accompanied by responsibilities to help the country prosper and to operate more effectively. Luisa's commitment in response to her newly acquired status as citizen illustrates this aspect of citizenship. In the case of the Philippians who lived in a Roman colony, they were expected to promote the interests of both the empire and their own city.

Paul's use of this analogy, which he applied to citizenship in heaven, illustrates something about the nature of our privileges and responsibilities as baptized persons. In comparing their heavenly citizenship to that of their own colony of Philippi in the Roman Empire, Paul's readers would understand that, as citizens of heaven who lived on earth, they were to promote the interests of Christ who made their heavenly citizenship possible. Christ's interests, as illustrated in the gospel, were to become their interests, and hence they would carry on the work of Christ in their own time. The earthly realm becomes the forum in which the follower of Christ is able to exercise partnership with Christ by making his love visible and tangible.

Christian citizenship implies that the baptized person

is a responsible member of the community of love that was called into being by Jesus and sealed by his resurrection. The author of the first letter of Peter characterizes Christians as a people of God:

> You are a chosen race, a royal priesthood, a holy nation, God's own people, that you may declare the wonderful deeds of the one who called you out of darkness into God's marvelous light. Once you were no people, but now you are God's people; once you had not received mercy, but now you have received mercy (1 Pet 2:9–10; RSV).

Christians are to bring hope to a world full of people in need of belonging. Authentic people of God make room for everyone from the lowest sinner to the holiest of the saints. Heavenly citizenship, therefore, does not render the Christian useless in this world. To the contrary, Christian citizenship embraces earthly citizenship as a medium for exercising partnership with Christ in transforming the world.

The Compassionate Citizen

Jesus is the model of compassion for the Christian citizen sojourning in the world. From the gospel, we learn to respond to the pain of God's people with the compassion of Jesus. The gospel frequently reflects the deep empathy and emotion that Jesus experienced in the face of sin and suffering. For example, the sight of a poor leper who was begging for healing touched Jesus deeply. "If you will," cried out the leper, "you can make me clean" (Mk 1:40–41). Mark tells us that Jesus was "moved with pity." The Greek word for "pity" or "compassion" (*splanchnizomai*) carries the connotation of a deep, gut-level emotion. Mark wants us to understand that the sight of a diseased person stirred Jesus to his very depths.

In Luke's account of "The Widow's Son," Jesus and

his disciples were approaching the town gate of Nain when they came upon a widow whose only son had died and was being carried out to the burial grounds. There was no social security system in first century Palestine, and widows with no children were among the most neglected in society. Jesus "had compassion on her" and raised her son from the dead (Lk 7:11–15). The same Greek word that expresses deep-seated feelings is also used in this passage. Jesus could not bear to see this poor woman with no one to care for her.

Again, when Jesus saw the hungry throng of five thousand, "he had compassion on them, because they were like sheep without a shepherd" (Mk 6:34). This same deep-felt emotion is expressed again when Jesus encounters a second crowd of four thousand people: "I have compassion for the crowd, because they have been with me now for three days and have nothing to eat" (Mk 8:2).

Throughout scripture, God is portrayed as constantly being concerned for the people. In the Old Testament, there are repeated echoes of God's mercy and love for us and indignation at injustice and oppression. In the New Testament, we hear from the compassionate heart of Jesus the "pathos of God"[1] even over a city whose leaders plotted against him:

> O Jerusalem, Jerusalem, killing the prophets and stoning those who are sent to you! How often would I have gathered your children together as a hen gathers her brood under her wings, and you would not (Mt 23:37–38; RSV).

As was always the case, God took the compassionate initiative toward these people. Their hearts, however, were hardened, and Jesus would not force them to respond.

As disciples of Jesus and citizens of God's reign, we too will experience within ourselves the pain of God's people on earth. If we allow Jesus and his love for others to nourish our spirituality, deep-felt compassion and emotion will stir us to prayer and action when we encounter the effects of sin, hunger, disease and homelessness in the lives of our brothers and sisters.

As Sheep Among Wolves

As citizens of two "worlds," the situation of Christians on earth is just as precarious as it was for Jesus. Jesus knew that his followers would have a difficult time, so in his prayer at the last meal before he died, he prayed especially for his disciples:

> The world has hated them because they do not belong to the world, just as I do not belong to the world.... As you have sent me into the world, so I have sent them into the world (Jn 17:14, 18).

The "world" referred to those people who were in opposition to the reign of God and God's servant in the world.

By living as followers of Jesus in our earthly society, Christians often become outsiders. Before Jesus left his disciples, he prepared them for rejection:

> If the world hates you, know that it hated me before you. If you were of the world, the world would love its own; but you are not of the world, because I chose you out of the world, therefore the world hates you. Remember the word that I said to you, "A servant is not greater than his master." If they persecuted me, they will persecute you; if they kept my word, they will keep yours also (Jn 15:18–20; RSV).

Hatred for the disciples springs from their association with Jesus. Because of the world's opposition, modern followers of Christ need support and encouragement from one another in the Christian community.

As citizens of heaven and ambassadors for Christ,

committed Christians seek to allow the gospel to govern
their decisions and actions. Jesus summarized for his followers one commandment that would enable them to
know what to do and to make God's love and compassion
a reality:

> You shall love the Lord your God with all your
> heart, and with all your soul, and with all your
> strength, and with all your mind; and your
> neighbor as yourself (Lk 10:27; RSV).

Love for God is tied to love of neighbor and self. We are
to take the needs of others as seriously as our own and
just as earnestly as our love for God.

A serious follower of Christ recognizes that no part
of life or the universe lies beyond the gracious concern
and love of God. The wounds of the world and its people
are a signal that the reign of God, for which Jesus sacrificed his life, is far from complete. The church's mission
in the world, then, is to extend the mercy and love of
God to the ends of the earth (Mt 28:19).

Prophetic Witnesses

As Christians, compassion may at times require that
we take a prophetic stance in our country of earthly citizenship. Abraham Heschel defined prophecy as "the
voice that God has lent to silent agony, a voice to the plun-
dered poor, to the profaned riches of the world.... [The
prophet] is a partner, an associate of God."[2] In the midst
of evil and oppression, the prophets spoke words of hope
even in situations that appeared hopeless. They assured
the people that God had not forsaken them, and they
spoke words of comfort in order to give them a sense of
God's care for them in their sufferings. The prophets also
helped the downtrodden focus on a future when God
would intervene on their behalf:

But you, O Bethlehem of Ephratha,
    who are one of the little clans of Judah,
from you shall come forth for me
    one who is to rule in Israel,
. . . .
And he shall stand and feed his flock
    in the strength of the Lord (Mic 5:2-4).

Through the Old Testament prophets, God also spoke words of judgment on those who oppressed the people:

The faithful have gone from the earth,
    among people, the upright are no more!
They all lie in wait to shed blood,
    each one ensnares the other.
Their hands succeed at evil,
    the prince makes demands,
The judge is had for a price....
The day of their...punishment has come,
    now their confusion is at hand (Mic 7:2-4; based on NAB).

Nevertheless, the prophets spoke of the triumph of God's mercy. They showed us that God's fidelity cannot be superseded by evil as reflected in the prophet's prayer:

Who is a God like you, pardoning iniquity
    and passing over the transgression
    of the remnant of your possession?
. . . .
You will show faithfulness to Jacob
    and unswerving loyalty to Abraham,
    as you have sworn to our ancestors
    from the days of old (Mic 7:18-20).

Jesus, God's living Word to us (Jn 1:1-4, 14), was perceived as a prophet by many people. When Jesus asked his disciples at Caesarea Philippi who people thought he

was, they answered: "John the Baptist; and others say,
Elijah; and others one of the prophets" (Mk 8:27–30; RSV).
It is not surprising that he was thought of as a prophet. In
Mark 7:1–23, Jesus was harassed by the Pharisees and
scribes because his disciples did not keep all the recom-
mendations of ritual cleansings before eating. Drawing
on the prophetic tradition of Isaiah, Jesus condemned the
hypocrisy of these religious leaders for belittling certain
commandments that came from God, while exacting
external observance of human traditions. Like the prophets of the Old Testament, he set the record straight about
what constituted authentic worship and what was useless
external sham that made life difficult for the poor.

Throughout his life, and especially by his rising from
the dead, Jesus brought hope to the world. In the face of
death, he made life a reality. He broke the power of death
so that even though the body die, we could live forever
with him. Sin, sickness, and disease, which separated
unfortunate people from the just in both religious and
social realms, were not the last word. By his forgiveness
and healings, Jesus showed us that they are only part of
the temporary world and not a factor in the reign of God.

Heralds of Hope

As citizens of heaven living on earth, our major
charge is to bring hope wherever we happen to be at the
moment. Just as Jesus spread hope in the midst of
despairing situations, every Christian thereafter has the
same mission of bringing hope. The hope we bring might
be visualized as a bridge that has its reference point in the
resurrection of Jesus and stretches over the present realities of life in this world to a future in which these realities
will be forever transformed. Paul acknowledges that we
hope for what we do not yet see (Rom 8:25). Our present
existence bears this out as we witness the victims of
crime, hunger, disease, war, and death. Nevertheless, even
in the midst of these devastating realities, the Christian is

challenged to bring the hope of Christ, the hope that things can be different because of Christ.

As followers and emissaries of the crucified and risen Jesus in the world, Christian citizens will speak God's word of hope to those who suffer. Whether in the slums of our big cities, at the bedside of suffering persons, or in the face of presumably impossible situations, Christians have a message and a mission of hope to offer the world.

St. Paul, in his letter to the Romans, addressed the relationship of a Christian to authority:

> Let every person be subject to the governing authorities. For there is no authority except from God, and those that exist have been instituted by God. Therefore, one who resists the authorities resist what God has appointed, and those who resist will incur judgment. For rulers are not a terror to good conduct, but to bad. Would you have no fear of him who is in authority? Then do what is good, and you will receive his approval, for he is God's servant for your good. But if you do wrong, be afraid, for he does not bear the sword in vain; he is the servant of God to execute his wrath on the wrongdoer (Rom 13:1-4).

Many people interpret Paul's admonition to the Roman church concerning authority as a mandate to blind obedience. But is Paul's intention to sanction all governing authorities regardless of their conduct? To understand the passage, two points bear consideration.

First, we need information about the historical situation out of which Paul's letter emerged. During this period of Roman history, the government under the leadership of Caesar Augustus had brought peace and security to the nations of the empire. Without doubt, the reign of peace enhanced the proclamation of the gospel to all the nations. (The letter to the Romans was written before the persecution of the Christians by Rome.) Paul probably understood this time of peace and tranquility as part of God's plan, indeed as ordained by God in order that the gospel might spread to all people. In this case, therefore, civil leaders should be respected and obeyed as servants of God.

Second, Paul believed that the endtime was in progress. This conviction may have persuaded him that it was best to live peacefully and respectfully with governing authorities, since they would soon be replaced by God's own rule.[3] In many ways, this passage is similar to the words of Jesus about what must be rendered to Caesar and what must be rendered to God (Mk 12:13-17). Both passages uphold civil authority, but always within the framework of a Christian's commitment to God.

Many baptized citizens question military service in view of the teachings of Jesus. The Mennonites, Brethren and Quakers have historically protested war and violence. They maintain that they are not bound by allegiance to any authority which advocates the taking of another's life. They have long been pressured by their local communities to be like everybody else and to serve their country in time of war. Before World War II, however, these churches were successful in getting Congress to pass legislation that allowed civilian public service as an alternative to military service. The government then approved another plan for overseas service projects in which conscientious objectors would serve the same period of time as military draftees. The United States Peace Corps developed out of this plan during the Kennedy administration.

These churches understand service to people in need as an expression of their religious belief that every baptized person is a servant of God and thus a servant to God's needy children. They view war in the context of Jesus' teaching that whatever we do to the least of our brothers and sisters, we do to him (Mt 25:40,45). Indeed, Christianity is a radical faith, "a faith not known according to its words, but according to the incarnate, embodied lives of those who bear its name."[4]

Being prophetic sometimes involves risks in regard

to one's profession, work, prestige or person. But Jesus warned those who followed him that they would be "as sheep among wolves" (Mt 10:16). Persecution could be expected, because "if they...called the master of the house Beelzebul, how much more would they malign those of his household" (Mt 10:25; RSV). Yet they were not to fear people who would falsely accuse them or even kill them. Nothing they could do to Christ's faithful ones could compare with the happiness awaiting them in eternity (Mt 5:11-12). Moreover, if God cares so much even for a simple sparrow, how much more does God care for us (Mt 6:25-30)?

Charting the Future

Justice and peace in the world, together with related concerns (i.e., hunger, homelessness, health care, etc.), are too complex today for Christians to limit their engagement in the world to individual acts of mercy, virtuous though they be. The political arena offers a channel through which a committed person can work in a more effective way with other people to chart the future for a better world community.

Modern society is in need of radical transformation in order to reflect more clearly the values that Jesus taught. Many important adjustments can be accomplished solely through the political system. Yet the political system depends on the electorate to make it functional.

People who are committed to the teachings of Jesus bring to the political arena a deep faith. They come to it with the compassion of Jesus to involve self, time, energy, talents and finances. They are "doers of the word and not merely hearers..." (Jas 1:22). Their baptismal vocation to love as Jesus did is lived out through their efforts to be the voice, the hands and the feet of the risen Jesus today. Authentic Christianity cannot be divorced from the realities of the world. Mary O'Connell maintains that

Christians who do not vote are not only lazy citizens but lazy Christians as well.[5]

Modern society is in need of radical transformation in order to reflect more clearly the values that Jesus taught. Many important adjustments can be accomplished solely through the political system. Yet the political system depends on the electorate to make it functional.

A great percentage of people who live in democracies do not exercise their right of suffrage. In the 1992 elections, only 55 percent of voters exercised their right to vote. In many cases, people never register to vote or else neglect to cast their ballot. Much of their malaise comes from the presumption that legislators and political leaders simply promote their own interests or those of their prominent benefactors.

Human genius has created a system of democracy wherein we can exercise authority over the earth by participative citizenship. One of the difficulties at the basis of many injustices is the fact that people have allowed their public officials to function independently. Once elections are over, all too many citizens remain inactive until it is time to vote again. They may not be satisfied with an official's performance regarding local, national, and world affairs, but often action is limited to private complaints and threats not to vote for the same person again.

The core of the problem does not appear to be inherent in democracy. In countries conducted by democratic systems, public officials are elected by the people. These officials likewise depend upon the electorate to remain in their positions. Elected officials who are interested in maintaining their positions try to respond to the wishes of their constituents who voice their opinions and vote. The crux of the issue for Christians, then, is that they examine public concerns and take action in light of the gospel: "My mother and my sisters and brothers are those who hear the word of God and do it" (Lk 8:21).

"Religion that is pure and undefiled before God," the author of the letter of James states, "is this: to visit orphans and widows in their afflictions and to keep oneself unstained from the world" (Jas 1:27; RSV). Orphans and widows are biblical stereotypes for the poor and powerless. We may not know personally many orphans and widows in our contemporary society, but almost everyone has some contact with impoverished people.

The greatest power of a nation resides within the citizens' right to vote. People have the power to affect not only the destiny of their own locality through elected representatives, but the destiny of the nation as a whole and consequently that of the entire planet. Power to bring about a better future can be achieved principally by informed, conscientious and responsible voting citizens. Neglect of suffrage has given rise to the scandalous incidents of injustices by leaders of many nations around the world. Thomas Jefferson sensed the value of the popular voice when he warned of the dangers of a passive electorate:

> Cherish...the spirit of your people and keep alive their attention.... If they become inattentive to public affairs, you and I, and Congress and Assemblies, Judges and Governors, shall all become wolves.[6]

Informed Citizenship

Being an informed citizen enables one to exercise voting power in a way that is aimed at effecting the common good. Becoming informed, however, requires devoting time to subjects that are generally less enticing than those offered for entertainment on TV and radio. Seeing, reading or hearing about the problems of the world can be extremely depressing if our perspective does not rise out of a hope-filled faith. Only then will we be able to watch with compassion the many sad realities of those people whom the gospel declares to be our brothers and sisters. Unless we know the reality, however, we cannot plan a course for change. The powerless and defenseless poor of our day depend on contemporary followers of Christ to live prophetically as did the pioneer who became God incarnate among us. We are their hope in the face of hopelessness. Therefore,

> Let us run with perseverance the race that is set before us, looking to Jesus the pioneer and perfecter of our faith, who for the joy that was set before him endured the cross, despising the shame... (Heb 12:1-2; RSV).

Only genuine love of ourselves and all other people can call forth the generosity and energy needed to make a difference. In his first letter to the Corinthians, St. Paul challenges the Christian who would retreat to complacency in the face of the world's suffering:

> If I speak in the tongues of people and of angels, but have not love, I am a noisy gong or a clanging cymbal. And if I have prophetic powers, and understand all mysteries and all knowledge, and if I have all faith, so as to remove mountains, but have not love, I am nothing. If I give away all I have, and if I deliver my body to be burned, but have not love, I gain nothing... Love bears all things, believes all things, hopes all things, endures all things (1 Cor 13:1-3, 7).

As a Christian, one cannot turn a deaf ear because of the trouble involved:

> If a brother or sister is ill-clad and in lack of daily food, and one of you says to them, "Go in peace, be warmed and filled," without giving them the things needed for the body, what does it profit (Jas 2:15-16; RSV)?

As we look around our neighborhoods, cities, country and the entire planet earth, the task of reversing inequity appears impossible and overwhelming. For example, how can we give all the needy people of the world the necessities of life, when perhaps we ourselves are struggling to provide for the needs of our own families? As Christians, however, we know that the impossible is possible in light of the resurrection of Jesus.

Impossible as the task may seem, Jesus assured us that things impossible for us are not so with God (Mk 10:27). Many Christians interpret this assurance as an invitation to leave the world's difficulties for God to solve. God, however, has given human beings intelligence and ingenuity with which to exercise stewardship over the earth. The many technical inventions are a tribute to the creativity that people have within them.

The gospel challenges people whose citizenship is in heaven to individual response to human needs, but it also calls for a more comprehensive approach to the problems of injustice in the world. Institutions, government structures and politics provide channels through which we are able to make inroads into systemic injustices that affect millions of people around the world.[7]

Letter writing is a forceful means of effecting change in practices or laws that do not promote the good of all and which ignore the standards of Jesus. Many people are unaware that the effectiveness of letters depends on the number of communications an elected official receives concerning an issue. For that reason, concerned citizens need to get organizations to which they belong (i.e., church and civic organizations, clubs, neighborhood groups, etc.) interested and knowledgeable. Once informed, these groups can set up a network that is astoundingly effective. Phone chains to keep members updated have been useful in many cases and have given many homebound persons an opportunity to be actively involved.

Such activities consume time and energy. Often the people most involved in civic responsibilities are already working full time, in addition to studying and caring for a family. Civic action, although an added burden to an already busy life, serves as a means of taking seriously St. Paul's analogy of the body as a symbol of those who are baptized:

> If one member suffers, all suffer together; if one member is honored, all rejoice together. Now you are the body of Christ and individually members of it (1 Cor 12:26-27).

The committed Christian will insist on the good of all people regardless of nationality, race or creed, a good based on justice, the rights of the poor, and freedom (but not license) for all people.

Once aware of the issues that affect people and our planet, one can move to active, cooperative and conscientious citizenship. Active Christian citizenship may necessitate making changes in our life-styles. Some of the changes will involve searching out and paying a little more for products safe for both human beings and the environment in order to halt the decline of our planet's health. Serious and informed citizens will refuse to buy things manufactured by companies that oppress its employees through underpayment, harassment, and unsafe working conditions. But self-sacrifice, as Paul reminds us, always involves a "self-emptying" in the likeness of Jesus:

> Have this mind among yourselves, which is yours in Christ Jesus, who, though he was in the form of God, did not count equality with God a thing to be grasped, but emptied himself, taking the form of a servant, being born in the likeness of humanity (Phil 2:5-7; RSV).

Another way to express this self-emptying is to say that God chose to assume the inconveniences and restrictions of being human. For us, being conscientious citizens also means living with the inconveniences and restrictions of a simple life-style in which waste of food and resources are minimized. More time and work will be involved in projects such as separating recyclable items for deposit or pick-up. Conscientious citizens will help inform other people about issues that affect the local, national, and international scene. They will call forth candidates for political offices who are knowledgeable, capable, honest and courageous to represent them and their values in government positions.

Summary

Christians, by reason of their baptism into the body of Christ, are citizens of two worlds—earth and heaven. As citizens of heaven and by reason of our baptism, we are called by Jesus to be his emissaries of hope in the world.

Christian citizenship is an effective means of exercising Jesus' command concerning neighborly love. Since we belong to the world community, we bear responsibility for its growth in goodness. The committed Christian who lives in a democracy has the opportunity to use the political system as a means of bringing about what is best for the global community. Voting with an informed conscience requires selfless denial of oneself in regard to time, energy and resources. Living the consequences of Christian citizenship is a risk that often entails hardship and personal loss. Nevertheless, authentic Christian life cannot be divorced from responsible citizenship.

The powerless and defenseless poor of our day depend on contemporary followers of Christ to live prophetically as did that pioneer who made God incarnate among us. We are their hope in the face of hopelessness.

As citizens of both worlds, the homeless (the subject of the following chapter) remind us to use the world's gifts judiciously in order that all people may enjoy the necessities of life.

For Further Reflection:

Rom 8:36–39
Mt 25:31–46
The gospel of Luke or Lk 9:57-62
1 Peter

SUGGESTED READINGS

Brueggemann, Walter. *Interpretation and Obedience.* Fortress, 1991.

Cahill, Lisa Sowle. "Religion and Political Life," *Theological Studies* 52 (March, 1991) 87–127.

Coleman, John Aloysius. "Two Pedagogies: Discipleship and Citizenship," *Education for Citizenship and Discipleship.* Edited by Mary Boys. Pilgrim Press, 1989, 59–61. "The Christian As Citizen," *Commonweal* 110 (September 9, 1983) 457–462.

Fahey, Joseph J. and Richard Armstrong, ed. *A Peace Reader. Essential Readings on War, Justice, Non-Violence and World Order.* Paulist, 1992.

Flynn, Eileen P. *My Country Right or Wrong? Selective Conscientious Objection in the Nuclear Age.* Loyola University Press, 1985.

Heschel, Abraham J. *The Prophets.* Harper and Row, 1962.

Kaylor, R. David. *Paul's Covenant Community: Jew and Gentile in Romans.* John Knox 1988.

Kirwin, S.J., Michael. "Faith in the Citizen: Poverty and the Citizenship Debate," *The Month* 251 (July, 1990) 282–286.

O'Connell, Mary. "The Least You Can Do Is Vote," *US Catholic* 52 (May, 1987) 14–16.

Slater, Nelle G. ed. *Tensions between Citizenship and Discipleship.* Pilgrim Press, 1989.

U.S. Catholic Conference Administrative Board, "Political Responsibility: Choices for the Future," *Origins* 17:21 (November 5, 1987).

3

Bridging the Abyss

Foxes have holes,
and birds of the air have nests,
but the Son of Man has nowhere to lay his head
(Lk 9:58; RSV).

A spirituality that emerges from reflection on sacred scripture perceives the abyss that separates the homeless from the rest of humanity as one that can be bridged. Because of the suffering of the homeless and the complexity of the problem, the process of linking the two worlds can be painful and frustrating. But in order to take our stand with Jesus as advocates for the homeless poor, we cannot avoid facing the reality that is theirs. By the very nature of the body of Christ, the experience of one member cannot be divorced from that of the whole body:

> If one member suffers, all suffer together; if one member is honored, all rejoice together. You are the body of Christ and individually members of it (1 Cor 12:26–27; RSV).

We might ask if the ordinary person has anything in common with the homeless people whose nights and days are spent in the streets of our cities and in the byways of our rural areas. God's word that comes to us in the New Testament contends that we do. We are all homeless. The first letter of Peter reminds Christians that we are on pilgrimage in this world, that this world is not our lasting home but rather the place of our journey to our eternal home. Jesus himself indirectly addressed our homelessness when he promised before his death that he would return to take us to himself (Jn 14:2-3).

Our homeless brothers and sisters shockingly and acutely demonstrate the transitory nature of our own sojourn in this world. In their painful condition, the homeless bring to our consciousness the fact that the new heaven and the new earth, in which there will be no more tears and no more death as spoken of in the book of Revelation (Rev 21:4), is still a future expectation. Unless we are willing to examine and embrace the situation of homelessness, we may easily dismiss that aspect of our social reality as unrelated to our spirituality.

God: Advocate for the Homeless

If we are serious about having been made in the image and likeness of God, we will look to scripture in order to emulate God's actions, attitudes and concerns as revealed to us. The ancient Israelites were an exploited and marginalized peasant people until God acted on their behalf. Israel was to remember that when God brought them out of slavery in Egypt, they were not abandoned. As the book of Deuteronomy asserts, God gave as unearned gift a land which provided housing and food for all (Dt 6:10-13) "in a world where none seemed available."[1] Israel was asked to do for others what God had done for them. They were to provide a safe refuge for those people who did not have security:

> You shall also love the stranger, for you were strangers in the land of Egypt (Dt 10:19).

The Old Testament prophet, Micah, was God's spokesperson for the homeless of his day. He lived and prophesied amidst an oppressed people in the small village of Moresheth in the Judean foothills, many of whom had lost their homes and land to greedy landlords. He cried out God's word against the wicked deeds of the powerful who spent their nights plotting to take advantage of the powerless:

> Woe to those who devise wickedness
>   and work evil upon their beds!
> When the morning dawns, they perform it,
>   because it is in the power of their hand.
> They covet fields and seize them;
>   and houses, and take them away.
> They oppress householder and house,
>   people and their inheritance (Mic 2:1-2; RSV).

When faced with the suffering of the poor, Micah did not mince words. He hurled harsh and bitter accusations at the leaders of the people who knew what was right. Instead of caring for God's powerless people, they metaphorically butchered them:[2]

> Should you not know justice?
>   you who hate the good and love the evil,
> who tear the skin off my people,
>   and their flesh off their bones;
> who eat the flesh of my people,
>   flay their skin off them (Mic 3:1-3).

Micah dramatically points out the inconsistency of religious worship which is not accompanied by justice. In that time and culture in ancient Israel, animal, grain and oil sacrifices were the major types of worship in the temple. The offering of these products from their farms was symbolic of their recognition that everything ultimately belongs to God, that they wished to be in good grace with God, and that they were sorry for their sins. But the prophet, Micah, speaks for God as he warns the Israelites that their offerings are empty of meaning if they do not treat others with love and justice. Micah poses questions that still make us ponder today whether our own generosity is acceptable to our God who emphatically expresses a desire for compassion and justice for the poor:

> With what shall I come before the Lord,
>> And bow myself before God on high?
> Shall I come before God with burnt offerings,
>> With calves a year old?
> Will the Lord be pleased with thousands of rams,
>> With ten thousands of rivers of oil?
> Shall I give my first-born for my transgression,
>> The fruit of my body for the sin of my soul?
> And what does the Lord require of you
>> But to do justice, and to love kindness,
>> And to walk humbly with your God (Mic 6:6-8).

In the New Testament, homelessness is not excluded from Jesus' experiences. In Luke's gospel, Jesus warns his followers that his own lot may be theirs also: "Foxes have holes, and birds of the air have nests; but the Son of man has nowhere to lay his head" (Lk 9:58; RSV). Jesus, a homeless person! Some people would call this an exaggeration on the part of the writer.[3]

However, in Lk 4:16-30, Jesus' own hometown people reject him and seek to throw him over a cliff. Later in the gospel, the writer tells us that on his way to Jerusalem, the Samaritan people refused to receive him into their village (Lk 9:51-53). The God who became human in order to show us the depths of God's love knows the pain of the dispossessed from firsthand experience.

In the gospel of Luke, Jesus recounts a story about a person who is similar to many of our homeless people today. The rich man's response in the story is not foreign to the experience of many contemporary street people.

> There was a rich man, who was clothed in purple and fine linen and who feasted sumptuously every day. And at his gate lay a poor man named Lazarus, full of sores, who desired to be fed with

what fell from the rich man's table; moreover the dogs came and licked his sores. The poor man died and was carried by the angels to Abraham's bosom. The rich man also died and was buried; and in Hades, being in torment, he lifted up his eyes, and saw Abraham far off and Lazarus in his bosom. And he called out, "Father Abraham, have mercy upon me, and send Lazarus to dip the end of his finger in water and cool my tongue; for I am in anguish in this flame." But Abraham said, "Son, remember that you in your lifetime received your good things, and Lazarus in like manner evil things; but now he is comforted here, and you are in anguish. And besides all this, between us and you a great chasm has been fixed, so that those who would pass from here to you would not be able, and none may cross from there to us." And he said, "Then I beg you, father, to send him to my father's house, for I have five brothers, so that he may warn them, lest they also come into this place of torment." But Abraham said, "They have Moses and the prophets; let them hear them." And he said, "No, Father Abraham; but if some one goes to them from the dead, they will repent." He said to him, "If they do not hear Moses and the prophets, neither will they be convinced if some one should rise from the dead" (Lk 16:19–31; RSV).

The rich man had lived a callous and self-centered life. Nothing moved him to compassion, not even the plight of a man lying covered with sores which the dogs licked. In first-century Palestine, it was customary to wipe one's hands with bread and then toss it under the table. The rich man would not even give Lazarus this hand-wiped bread. After his death, the rich man cried out to his spiritual ancestor, Abraham, for mercy, but the time for mercy had passed. He then begged that his brothers be warned so that they might escape similar punishment. Abraham, however, replied that if they did not listen to the warnings of the prophets, neither would a miracle turn their hearts to justice.

We need only to walk the streets of our cities in order to see countless modern Lazaruses. Given the situation that continues to exist, we need to ask ourselves if we are any less callous than the rich man in the parable. If our closets bulge with clothing that is neither worn nor needed; if our tables display an abundance of rich foods, much of which is wasted without thought of hungry street people; if our worship seldom gives thought to injustices, we are falling short of living in the image and likeness of God.

Alan Paton expresses well the connection between the gospel and justice:

> Love without justice is a Christian impossibility, and can only be practiced by those who have divorced religion from life, who dismiss a concern for justice as "politics" and who fear social change much more than they fear God.[4]

Faith needs to be a faith of love, and love is not an abstraction; it must be expressed in a concrete way. In the letter of James, there is a warning about separating faith from concern for others:

> If a brother or sister is ill-clad and in lack of daily food, and one of you says to them, "Go in peace, be warmed and filled," without giving them the things needed for the body, what does it profit? (Jas 2:15–16; RSV).

Homeless Gift the Home-ful

"It took the homeless to bring us all together," wrote Fr. Tony Philpot of Cambridge, England.[5] At first,

Cambridge students, area churches, and other organizations tried individually to address the issue of homelessness. In spite of all their efforts, the problem continued to mushroom.

Finally, representatives of the various groups, and some of the homeless people from the streets around Cambridge, held a meeting to discuss future involvement. One person in the group told of a French priest, Abbé Pierre, who had started Emmaus communities for the homeless all over France. An Emmaus community was a home for homeless people which was attached to a recycling enterprise that maintained the house and its residents. The people became independent and were able to regain their self-esteem in addition to having a kind of family or community support. The Cambridge area group made a bold decision to establish the first Emmaus community in England in 1991.

After experiencing initial failures and struggles in getting the program off the ground, they were able to get Cambridge area community support and began making concrete plans for their first house. Emmaus International sent consultants; the 78 year-old Abbé Pierre himself arrived unexpectedly; and the project was helped by an increasing number of supportive people.

Finally, property was purchased, and an administrator, responsible for the business aspects and community life in the house, was hired. He began recruiting people from the streets, along with skilled and unskilled volunteers, to renovate the buildings. At last, about one year later, England's first Emmaus community opened its doors. Tony Philpot realized, however, that no matter how good the concept of Emmaus was, a community was not the solution to all homelessness:

> Not all the homeless will like the philosophy of Emmaus (that once you are one degree clear of destitution, your first thought must be for those at the bottom of the pile). For many—active alco-

holics, drug addicts, congenital loners—other means of help have to be found. Emmaus is a tiny palliative.

But, like Martin Luther King, we have a dream. It is that other towns and cities will attempt to start Emmaus, and be delighted, as we have been, by the degree of backing they receive simply because Emmaus is new, and has within it a sturdy, stubborn independence and determination that the poor and homeless shall once again stand on their own two feet, be beholden to no welfare system, and be able to look the rest of the world in the eye.[6]

In this country, Habitat for Humanity International, an ecumenical Christian housing organization, has made a significant contribution to resolving the problem of homeless families. The project involves individuals and groups who try to provide an alternative to temporary family housing. Habitat for Humanity works with already existing parallel agencies so as not to duplicate efforts. The organization relies upon both skilled and unskilled volunteer labor to build adequate and simply designed houses from donated materials. Habitat then sells the houses to low-income families at a reduced cost. The families have twenty years to pay the mortgage, without interest.[7] Families themselves are asked to donate a certain number of work-hours toward building their own house or that of another.

These stories are among the many that could be told about Christians who take seriously Jesus' statement that deeds done to others are done to him (Mt 25:40). Such initiatives are witness to what dedication to gospel values can do, not only for the homeless, but especially for those who overcome the human tendency to ignore that which seems beyond human capacity to solve. Undoubtedly, the Christian concern of both the Cambridge group and those who promote Habitat for Humanity stems from a spirituality based on Jesus' way of responding to human need. That spirituality was contagious, and it spread to many people who perhaps had never thought of getting involved in the lives of the homeless.

Stories like this fill us with hope in the midst of a desperate situation with which almost every city and country has to deal. We need those rays of hope in order to realize that the power of Christ's resurrection and victory over evil is indeed operative today. But in order to avoid basking in success stories alone and forgetting the reality, we need to look at the sad and less inspirational accounts that witness to the work that is yet to be done.

In a Mirror Dimly

On March 14, 1991 at 5:45 a.m., a stray dog was run over and killed by a subway train in a large city. 75,000 riders on sixty-three trains were delayed for four hours while a search for the dog was conducted. There was an immediate clamor against the motorman for having run down a poor helpless little dog. The tragedy was the subject of reports by all the news media. Two days later, *The New York Times* carried a lengthy article with the caption, "Two Criminal Summonses After a Dog Dies Beneath a Train."[8] The humane society, after receiving hundreds of calls, issued summonses against the motorman and the Transit Authority which carried a maximum penalty of $1,000 and a year in jail. Some of the phone callers threatened to kill the motorman if they could identify him. The last sentence of the article casually mentioned that two people had been killed by the subway trains in the last twenty-four hours.

On the next page opposite the end of the account of the dog's death, there appeared an article entitled "New Delay in Hotel Plan for Homeless." Fortunately, there were no reports of death threats as in the case of the unfortunate dog's death. There were no reprisals against those responsible for the alleged incompetence which brought the long delay in the housing for homeless people. Failure to go forward with the shelter for the homeless obviously was not considered high on the list of human interest stories. By no means did it engage the same special attention by the media as did the story of the dog's death on the subway. Certainly, the housing delay did not call forth widespread protests on behalf of the poor people who remained without shelter. Neither were the persons who were accused of irresponsibility in the matter issued summonses that carried fines and jail sentences.

There were no reports of people jamming telephone lines (as in the case of the dog) wanting to know what had caused the subway trains to run over two people. Likewise, there were no demands for details about the identity, nor the exact time or place of the deaths of the two people killed by subway trains. But the silent voice of God was crying out from the pages of the scriptures against indifference.

> Because you trample
>   on the poor...
> Although you have built houses of
>   hewn stone,
> you shall not live in them....
> I know how many are your
>   transgressions,
>   and how great are your sins—
> you who afflict the righteous...
>   and push aside the needy in the gate...
> Seek good and not evil
>   that you may live (Amos 5:11–12, 14).

All life is sacred, whether it be a stray dog or a human being, and unnatural death should rouse the sympathy and concern of the community. Nevertheless, when one compares public response to the death of the dog with that of the two human beings and the situation of the homeless, the inconsistency shown indicates something alarming about values in society at large. It appears that we still "see in a mirror dimly" (1 Cor 13:12).

During the last decade, "street people" have become increasingly more numerous. At the same time, more and more people are becoming intolerant of them and are pressing politicians to get them out of sight. Nobody knows how many homeless people there are in the United States. Estimates range from a quarter of a million to three million.[9]

Faceless Persons

Persons who are labeled "the homeless" are all too often without names or faces. If we are to relate faith to the reality of homelessness, it is imperative that we identify the homeless. Only then can we embrace them as companions on our spiritual journey and hear the lessons that they in their homelessness can teach us.

In spite of their appearances and anonymity, each homeless person is someone's son or daughter, one of our brothers or sisters in Christ. Homeless people are young and old, men and women, teenagers, young children and babies. Their faces are all shades of black and white. The homeless represent almost every race and every religious creed, as well as atheists and agnostics. They come from families of prestigious backgrounds, from middle-class society, and from the economically poor. We find the homeless in our cities, suburbs, and rural America.

Some homeless people are mentally healthy, others are not; some are lazy, while others are ambitious. Many are the victims of AIDS, whose families have disowned them or whose medical expenses have left them penniless. Some homeless persons are addicted to drugs, while others have always been drug-free. A few of them choose to live on the streets; most of them are there by necessity. Many of the homeless are educated, while others lack schooling. They are teachers, honor students, artists, musicians and playwrights. Others are plumbers, electricians and carpenters. The homeless are war heroes, down-and-out veterans and disabled persons. They are ex-convicts and lifelong honest people. Some are homeless individuals, while others are homeless families. They are people who have lost their homes because medical bills wiped out their savings. A significant number of homeless individuals are employed, but they do not earn enough to pay rent.

The homeless sleep on park benches, under cardboard boxes, in tents and cars, near air vents and in gutters. They have feelings; they want to be treated with dignity; they hurt; they cry, and they laugh. Homeless people are human beings just as we are. They represent a cross section of society, and they are our brothers and sisters. They belong to the family of God; with Jesus they, too, have God as their "Abba" (Rom 8:14–17). Yet in spite of these relationships,

> [t]he homeless are aliens in their own land....
> Many homeless are virtually helpless. They have
> no address and cannot qualify for public assis-
> tance.... You can see in their faces that for many it
> is just as awkward and embarrassing to ask for
> help as it would be for any of us to ask for help.[10]

The homeless are probably the most misunderstood sector of our society. They are often looked upon as lazy parasites, content with their wanderings and freeloading. Little do critics realize that many of them are unable to get or hold employment. Sharon Curtin calls the struggles of a homeless bag lady a "full time job." One woman explained that she cannot seek shelter in any one welfare hotel for too long. If she did, the junkies would find out, steal her checks and possibly even kill her. Every time she moves, she must make three trips to the welfare office for approval of a new place, "even if it's just another cockroach-filled, rat-infested hole in the wall."[11]

Most street people work hard in order to survive.

The hassles they must endure are countless. One homeless person was told by a welfare worker that she could get food stamps. After the poor woman waited in line for three hours, she was informed that she was not eligible since she did not have cooking facilities in her room. Standing in lines constituted her social life:

> I run around the city and stand in line... I stand in line for medicine, for food, for glasses, for the cards to get pills, for the pills.... I stand in line at the hotels, sometimes I even have to stand in line to go to the john. When I die there'll probably be a line through the gate, and when I get up to the front of the line, somebody will push it closed and say, "Sorry. Come back after lunch."[12]

Searching for a Solution

Regardless of who the homeless are, the basic cause of their homelessness is lack of housing. They may have come to the streets because of alcoholism, family breakdown, poverty, drugs, or a variety of other reasons, but they remain on the streets simply because there is not enough habitable housing.[13]

Once people have lived in motels for the homeless, it is hard to get an apartment. They often leave the motels addicted to drugs, and often they carry roach-infested belongings. Life in a motel frequently creates a never-ending tunnel of dependence for the homeless.

> Homelessness creeps over its victims like T.S. Eliot's yellow smoke. First, you recognize that something is wrong in your life and suddenly you—and maybe your family too—are on the streets. You're in shock. It's a catastrophe to you, but nobody else seems to notice. And death— early, gratuitous and unnecessary—creeps in too. It's as common to those people who live in the

streets as that studied glance away most
Americans instinctively develop when a homeless person appears in their path.... There is no
national cemetery with neat rows of white tomb-
stones for the army of the homeless. In death
comes the final, and typical indignity: a crude
burial with dozens of other corpses in an open
trench in some windswept Potter's Field.[14]

Brian Hehir bases his plea for respectable housing for
the homeless on human rights. In an address to a sub-
committee of the Senate Banking, Housing and Urban
Affairs Committee, he emphasized the right of every
human being to have proper shelter:

[D]ecent and affordable housing for every man,
woman and child is a basic human right, one
that flows from the dignity of the human person.
That principle implies a mandate for each one of
us and for society as a whole—a mandate to
ensure that in the richest nation on earth, no one
should go without adequate shelter.[15]

As early as 1975, the bishops in the United States issued a
pastoral letter that called for a cooperative response to
the problem of inadequate housing. They stressed the
dignity and worth of every individual "because he or she
is created in the image of God."[16] The bishops emphasized that the right to a decent home is based on that
divinely bestowed dignity of each person. They emphasized our individual moral responsibility to act and the
need to effect "structural policies and practices"[17] that
would lead to a solution.

At the same conference, the bishops called the
church to examine its resources—"land, economic and
personnel resources." They recommended that these
assets be utilized to resolve the housing crisis. They
warned that "the one thing we cannot do is to acknowl-

edge the immoral situation of indecent, inadequate housing and do nothing about it."[18]

Close to two decades have passed since the publica-
tion of the bishops' document, and significant progress
has been made. Many churches have turned their base-
ment facilities into soup kitchens and temporary shelters
for the homeless. Local church organizations, such as
committees for social justice, have adopted homeless
families and linked up with regional civic efforts to alleviate the housing crisis. These are noble endeavors, but
the concerted efforts of every church and every civic
group in the country is needed in order to help halt the
growing and critical problem of homelessness.

A lasting solution to the problems of inadequate
housing, however, requires a united effort from both the
private and public sectors. Churches and neighborhoods
can negotiate with private developers for respectable and
affordable housing that does not diminish the value of
already existing property. "Low-cost housing, which the
occupants can eventually own rather than rent,"[19] can
prevent the problem of lack of maintenance. Organized
groups as well as individuals can work with financial
institutions and all levels of government to reach attain-
able goals. With assessment of job skills and local needs,
churches and local civic groups could put many homeless people back to work and give them the opportunity
to regain their dignity. Jobs are essential, and thus job
training needs to be provided for persons able to work.

There are practical things that can be done to help
resolve the problem of homelessness. But first of all, it is
necessary to be informed about the problem. Nothing is
as valuable as firsthand experience. A visit to a shelter or
transitional home can provide the stimulus to become
better informed. Reading about the homeless and the
problem of shelter in newspapers and periodicals keeps
one abreast of the issues and gives one a background to
discuss the situation with other people.

Getting acquainted with a homeless person has the

potential of breaking down stereotypes. Giving homeless people a nod or a greeting with eye-to-eye contact can help one realize the fact that they are indeed human beings, persons who, for the most part, have met their misfortune through no fault of their own. Often the desperation in the eyes of those who are cold and hungry is enough to make the words of Jesus ring loud and clear:

> Truly I tell you, just as you did it to one of the least of these who are members of my family, you did it to me (Mt 25:40).

Passing street people by as if they were not there is only a means of squelching compassion and hardening our hearts to reality.

Volunteering services to agencies and getting church and civic groups involved is another step in the direction of solving problems related to homelessness. Some of the people who are most committed to seeking solutions began their quest with volunteer work in soup kitchens or other service centers that provide food and shelter. This kind of volunteer work is especially good for young people who would benefit from seeing the harder side of life.

There is a need for volunteers to tutor children in shelters and a need for professionals to assist in the areas of social work, medicine, and law. Countless persons end up homeless because they do not know their legal rights. Others are unaware of available aid or how to obtain it. Many homeless people do not read or write, so they never return forms that they once received to fill out. It is not easy to acknowledge that one is illiterate. These situations are some that many of us are qualified to help alleviate.

Most of all, voters have the opportunity to impress upon legislators, local and national, how important they consider the need for adequate shelter. Letters that indicate a grasp of the extent of homelessness and carry the demand that something be done are effective to officials who wish to remain in office. Requests that legislative

newsletters report on progress made in this area of interest have the potential to ignite action in congress. Our
public officials know that they hold office because of our
votes,[20] and silence regarding issues signals contentment
with the status quo.

The extraordinary advances in technology and the
high standard of living in parts of our world today

> seem only to heighten and intensify the excruci-
> ating and dehumanizing experiences of men
> and women of today's world where 3 percent of
> the population is still consuming over 60 per-
> cent of the world's wealth. The 1990 World
> Development Report, issued by the World Bank,
> estimates "that more than 1 billion people,
> roughly a fifth of the earth's human population,
> are currently living at the most desperate
> extremity of poverty—struggling to survive on
> less than $370 a year." Such deprivation of the
> necessities of life itself amid an affluent and
> comfortable society can only embrace the hor-
> rors of war and the exploitation of peoples to
> satiate the greed and power of a few.[21]

This comparison of the wealth of a few people with that of
many is reminiscent of ancient Israel's greed in the midst
of the homelessness of a great number of God's people:

> Ah, you who join house to house,
>   who add field to field,
>   until there is room for no one but you,
>   and you are left to live alone
>   in the midst of the land!
> The lord of Hosts has sworn in my hearing:
>   Surely many houses shall be desolate,
>   large and beautiful houses,
>   without inhabitant (Is 5:8–10).

Some affluent homeowners were grabbing up land from the powerless poor and depriving them of a place to live.

Summary

A spirituality based upon our biblical tradition reflects God's concern for the homeless and challenges us to act in the image and likeness of God. The homeless are a reminder to us that our real home is in heaven. They challenge us to root ourselves in the gospel, to count material things as little, and to treat others as we would treat Jesus.

"The homeless" is a label which tends to put a facade over the faces of the human persons involved. A label makes it easy to forget that they are human beings like ourselves. They are people who suffer and rejoice and experience all the emotions we do, and who want to be treated with dignity. They are persons who face death in the open streets of dangerous sections of the city in a way that most of us will never know.

Homeless people are not a modern phenomenon; both the Old and New Testaments call for compassion and justice for these unfortunate persons of society. Our Judeo-Christian tradition calls for justice based on the dignity of each person as a human being created to God's own image and likeness. The situation of homeless people on the streets of the United States, the wealthiest nation in the world, has drawn the attention of people around the globe. To people of other countries, homelessness in a wealthy nation is almost inconceivable. To American citizens, it is a growing problem that many people work toward solving, and still too many others ignore or look for superficial solutions. But anyone who would be a disciple of Christ will search for ways to bring about a more humane social system and will become part of the solution according to one's own means whether by prayer, active involvement or both.

Closely related to the homeless are immigrants who come to the United States seeking refuge from persecution or a better life. Their lives reflect our own sojourn on this earth. The following chapter invites us to embrace the alien as a companion on our journey.

For Further Reflection:

Job 24
Ps 112
Amos
Ezek 34:11-16

SUGGESTED READINGS

Bard, Marjorie. *Shadow Women. Homeless Women's Survival Stories*. Sheed and Ward, 1990.

Brueggemann, Walter. "The Practice of Homefulness," *Journal for Preachers* 15, 4 (1992) 7-22.

Grady, Duane. *Helping the Homeless: God's Word in Action*. Brethren Press, 1988.

Hehir, J. Brian. "Homelessness Today—And Tomorrow," *Origins* 16 (February 26, 1987) 656-659.

Johnson, Joan J. *Kids without Homes*. Franklin Watts, 1988.

Johnson, M. E. and S. Brewer, "Good News for the Homeless," *New Choices for the Best Years* 30 (July, 1990) 9.

Kim, E. Kon. "'Outcry' Its Context in Biblical Theology," *Interpretation* 42 (1988) 229-239.

Kozal, Jonathan. *Rachel and Her Children: Homeless Families in America*. Crown Publishers, 1988.

Kraljic, Matthew A., editor. *The Homeless Problem*. H. W. Wilson & Company, 1992.

Stavsky, Lois and J. E. Mozeson, *The Place I Call Home: The Faces and Voices of Homeless Teens*. Shapolsky Publishers, 1990.

Stoner, Madeleine R. *Inventing a Non-Homeless Future: A Public Agenda for Preventing Homelessness*. Peter Lang Publishing, 1989.

What Have You Done To Your Homeless Brother? The Church and the Housing Problem. Document of the Pontifical Commission "Iustitia et Pax" on the Occasion of the International Year of Shelter for the Homeless (Vatican City: 1987).

4

Encountering the Alien

The alien who resides with you
shall be to you as a citizen among you;
you shall love the alien as yourself (Lev 19:34).

He was an alien. He looked like us, and he spoke like us. But he was an alien. He couldn't make them understand. "He came unto his own," the gospel of John tells us, "but his own people did not receive him" (Jn 1:11). When he said he was from above, the religious leaders scoffed at him. They didn't like it that an alien was telling them what God was really like—loving, forgiving, accepting of every person. Finally, when they could take him no longer, they crucified him. He died, an alien, away from his home, some two thousand years ago.

Hope for the Hopeless

Today, planes glide down runways after miles of cross-ocean flights, ships pull up to docks, flimsy boats brave the last threatening wave. From all of them, weary immigrants carefully place one foot and then another on the hope-filled soil of freedom. Their eyes sparkle with tears as they reach Ellis Island and hear the silent voice of the great woman of liberty, holding high the torch of freedom:

> Give me your tired, your poor,
> Your huddled masses yearning to breathe free,
> The wretched refuse of your teeming shore.
> Send these, the homeless, tempest-tost to me,
> I lift my lamp beside the golden door!

This touching scene is repeated every day around the globe, especially in the United States. But does the exhilarating drama of the initial arrival of immigrants to our American soil match the reality of their extended existence in our land of freedom and opportunity? That is the dilemma that clouds the minds of many people who echo the haunting question posed by Rodney King during the 1992 Los Angeles riots: "Can we all get along?"

Our Judeo-Christian tradition is marked by centuries of both callousness and regard for peoples of other nations. In the Old Testament, ancient Israel constantly came into contact with one culture after another. At times and in many ways, the Israelites rejected other people unlike themselves just as we often do. On the other hand, there were instances in which they appreciated other peoples.

In the book of Job, a person is judged either good or evil by the way he or she behaves toward the powerless (Job 31:16–32; also Ps 94:6). The well-being of a community is measured by how well the widow, the orphan, and the sojourner are treated (Ezek 22:7).[1] In the Old Testament, immigrants were often placed alongside widows, orphans, and sojourners because of their vulnerability to oppression (cf. Lev 19:10; 23:33; Job 29:12–13; Is 10:2). Like many people in multicultural communities today, they didn't blend in socially since they looked and spoke differently from the other people.

Welcoming the Stranger

Hospitality to a stranger in the Old Testament frequently became hospitality to God. Abraham, a nomadic tent-dweller, considered it a "favor" that he had the opportunity to render hospitality to strangers. They arrived unexpectedly. Abraham did not know that they were messengers from God; yet he honored them by "bending down" before them and welcoming them to share his table (Gen 18:1–8). Concerning this surprise visit, Claus

Westermann writes: "The visit of a stranger could be of vital, decisive importance for the one visited,"[2] because the dignity of the stranger may be camouflaged by external appearances.

The people of Sodom present a powerful contrast to Abraham's hospitality in Genesis 19. Abraham's nephew, Lot, extended hospitality to two strangers who, unbeknown to Lot, were angels. The strangers intended to sleep in the town square, but Lot prevailed upon them to spend the night in his house (Gen 19:2). The citizens of Sodom, however, would have sexually abused the strangers had God not intervened. The townspeople resented Lot's attempt to protect them. "This fellow," they sneered, "came here as an immigrant, and now he dares to give orders" (Gen 19:1-11). Even today, "Sodom and Gomorrah" continue to be metaphors for crimes of inhumanity to others.[3]

In general, the laws regarding hospitality were extended only to males in the society of the ancient Near East. A widow in the ancient Near East was in a vulnerable situation, especially if she had no children. The book of Ruth gives us a story of Israelite hospitality extended to a female who was both an alien and a widow. When Ruth's husband died, she left her native country of Moab and went with her widowed Jewish mother-in-law to Bethlehem of Judah.

Boaz, a Bethlehemite of some means, was a model host to the alien widow. He not only offered Ruth hospitality, but he also gave her the privilege of working with the Israelite community in a protective atmosphere.[4] Boaz said to Ruth:

> Do not glean in another field or leave this one, but keep close to the young women. I have ordered the young men not to bother you. If you get thirsty, go to the vessels and drink from what the young men have drawn (Ruth 2:8-9).

Clearly, Boaz went beyond the demands of the Law regarding aliens. He was attentive to Ruth's unspoken needs, and he was sensitive to her lack of familiarity with the Israelite foods and manner of eating.

> At mealtime Boaz said to her, "Come here, and eat some of this bread, and dip your morsel in the sour wine." So she sat beside the reapers, and he heaped up for her some parched grain. She ate until she was satisfied, and she had some left over (Ruth 2:14-15).

According to the law, the poor had the right to glean whatever was left in the fields after the harvest. Much of the time, this right depended on the good will of the owner. But Boaz not only obeyed the law, he even allowed Ruth to glean while the harvesters were still at work. Moreover, without her knowing it, he arranged with his workers to leave some of the sheaves standing for her.

> When she got up to glean, Boaz instructed his young men, "Let her glean even among the standing sheaves, and do not reproach her. You must also pull out some handfuls for her from the bundles, and leave them for her to glean, and do not rebuke her." So she gleaned in the field until evening (Ruth 2:15-17).

Boaz, therefore, showed respect for Ruth's dignity. He could have given her the sheaves, but instead, she was allowed to work for her sustenance. Working among Boaz' people also gave both her and the workers the opportunity to get to know one another.

A spirituality that embraces aliens today will be mindful of the difficulties that they face in a new culture. They need friendly, welcoming people to introduce them to family, friends, and available local resources. They also need people like Boaz to help them maintain their dignity as they make their transition into a whole new world.

Remembering Our Roots

The history of the people of Israel began with their existence as aliens in a foreign land. The Exodus event came about because of Egypt's oppression of the Israelites. This people first migrated to Egypt in a time of famine when Joseph (who had been sold into slavery by his brothers) basked in the Pharaoh's favor because of his ability to interpret dreams. For many years, they enjoyed hospitality, peace, and security in a foreign land. As time passed, however, another Egyptian Pharaoh feared the Israelites and forced them into slavery, because he saw how they multiplied and prospered.

> Therefore they set taskmasters over them to oppress them with forced labor.... The Egyptians became ruthless in imposing tasks on the Israelites, and made their lives bitter (Ex 1:11-13).

So bitter was the sojourners' slavery that God intervened and delivered them under the leadership of Moses. Once God liberated the Israelites from slavery and they had their own land, they never forgot to care for the aliens who came to them. They promulgated laws to protect the foreigners and other powerless people.[5]

Israel's sacred writings attest that its people never forgot their roots as aliens: "A wandering Aramean was my ancestor; he went down into Egypt and lived there as an alien" (Dt 26:5). Part of ancient Israel's population consisted of resident aliens, people who lived within the community but did not have political rights.[6] The Deuteronomic law, however, provided for their protection. Israel considered that the fields they harvested belonged to God:

> The land shall not be sold in perpetuity, for the
> land is mine and you are strangers and sojourn-
> ers with me (Lev 25:23; RSV).

The people were to be compassionate to those who
had no legal right to the community's wealth:

> You shall not withhold the wages of poor and
> needy laborers, whether other Israelites or aliens
> who reside in your land in one of your towns.
> You shall pay them their wages daily before sun-
> set, because they are poor and their livelihood
> depends on them; otherwise they might cry to
> the Lord against you, and you would incur guilt
> (Dt 24:14-15).

The Israelites understood that had it not been for God's
mercy, they would still be living in a foreign land. From
their experience as aliens, they knew their God to be a
vindicator of the poor, the weak, and the helpless, and
that God demanded the same of them. According to the
prophet Jeremiah, justice to the powerless was a prereq-
uisite for God's abiding presence among the people (Jer
7:5–7).

The harvest was not to be stripped clean of all its
fruit, because the poor needed to glean food to eat.

> When you reap the harvest of your land, you
> shall not reap to the very edges of your field, or
> gather the gleanings of your harvest; you shall
> leave them for the poor and for the alien: I am
> the Lord your God (Lev 23:22).

One biblical scholar refers to this practice of caring for
the needs of the poor as Israel's "social security system."[7]

Legally, aliens were entitled to the same justice as
the Israelites: "Give the members of your community a
fair hearing, and judge rightly between one person and

another, whether citizen or resident alien" (Dt 1:16). The Edomites, descendants of Esau, who had often waged war against them, and the Egyptians who had previously enslaved the Israelites, were at the mercy of their hosts. But the law commanded inclusion even of their past enemies:

> You shall not abhor any of the Edomites, for they are your kin. You shall not abhor any of the Egyptians, because you were an alien residing in their land (Dt 23:7).

Foreigners were also to be included in the festivals worshipping Yahweh, and care was to be given to those who might have been most despised.

A Tapestry of Cultures

The forms of many of our Christian traditions come from cultures that antedate Christianity. Our spiritual ancestors were able to see value in such cultural aspects as literature, song, and art. They often adapted the literature and song of other nations as vehicles to communicate their theology. For example, the Gilgamesh epic (an ancient Babylonian story which deals with immortality, good and evil) is thought to be the basis for the composition of the second creation story (Gen 2:4–3:24).[8] The author simply took a story known in that part of the world, and in view of the contrasts between Yahweh and the pagan gods, he adapted the story and its characters to express God's self-revelation to us. The Psalms, one of Israel's expressions of faith in God, have their setting in the culture of the ancient Near East. Some scholars believe that Psalm 29 was a Canaanite hymn that the Israelites adapted to the praise of the one God.[9]

New Testament writers also manifest an awareness of cultural practices of different people in mixed populations. Paul, as well as the authors of the gospels, had to adapt the message of Jesus to multicultural communities. Jesus' audience was almost always Jewish, but after the resurrection, the gospel spread far beyond the borders of Palestine. The New Testament writings reveal the struggle in the early church as it dealt with the first multicultural Christian communities.

On the day of Pentecost, when the Holy Spirit came to the community, the people present from all over the world heard the apostles speaking in their own languages (Act 2:6). Nationality was no hindrance to communication. When the Spirit of love is allowed to transform a group or neighborhood, differences in customs and language can actually unite them in mutual determination to build a community of acceptance and love.

The early church not only embraced the pain of the alien, but it also valued and incorporated the cultural differences of its members into its own. New members were not forced to abandon their culture and forget their identity. Efforts on the part of the early Christians to respect people of different origins are reflected in the account of the Jerusalem Council (Gal 2:1–10; Acts 15:1–10). Paul persuaded them that the Jewish practice of circumcision should not be forced upon his non-Jewish converts since that practice was not necessary for salvation. Hence, Titus a Greek Gentile convert, was not compelled to submit to Jewish customs unessential to the Christian faith. He was allowed to maintain his cultural dignity, which in no way compromised his faith.

In another instance, Peter, the church leader, was shown in a vision that Jewish dietary laws were canceled so as not to inhibit the spread of the gospel to the Gentiles (Acts 10:9–16). Later, on entering the house of Cornelius, a Gentile, Peter explained that God had revealed to him "not to call any person common or unclean" (Acts 10:28). This was clearly a direction in which Christianity was to move, because in Christ, neither nationality, nor creed, nor any other division can endure. "He is our peace, who has made us both one, and has broken down the dividing wall of hostility" (Eph 2:14). The Lord's supper was the symbol of unity that brought their diversity into Christian focus.

The author of the letter to the Hebrews counsels his readers: "Do not neglect to show hospitality to strangers, for thereby some have entertained angels unawares" (Heb 13:2; RSV). According to sociological studies, the first letter of Peter is thought to be addressed to aliens in the Christian communities of Asia Minor. The encouragement given in the letter seems to indicate that the addressees were suffering the effects of living in a foreign land.[10] According to the author, those who are regarded as strangers and social outcasts by their host country need not feel ostracized. Their home is the Christian community, the church.

The dispirited disciples on the way to Emmaus were unaware that they were entertaining the risen Jesus in the stranger who joined them on the way. They shared with him what had been going on in their city and even their own feelings of dejection over the death of Jesus. They offered him hospitality, and it was in sharing their table that they recognized who the stranger was (Lk 24:13-35). How differently the story might have ended had they not been hospitable to the one who apparently was a stranger in Jerusalem.

People of various cultures bring a richness to the church and to society that cannot be achieved otherwise. Immigrants bring to a community new ways of thinking, praying, facing the difficulties of life, and extending love to the community. Only when there is an atmosphere of mutual acceptance and trust can these gifts be shared. The dialogue between faith and culture, or "inculturation," can take place only when people sincerely believe that "those who do not love a brother or sister whom they have seen, cannot love God whom they have not seen" (1 Jn 4:20).

"Melting Pot" or "Stew Pot"

At the present time, ours is a country populated by almost every race and nation. The image of a "melting pot" has frequently been used to describe this phenomenon. The concept of a "melting pot," however, would seem to indicate that differences dissolve. Yet, from the beginning of colonialization until the present, there has been no blending of vision, no gentle flow of a multicultural stream. Reality defies a picture of racial amalgamation and assimilation. Our law books witness to the history of struggle which the different races have endured in order to live in this country.

The so-called "melting pot" that our ancestors sought to create obviously reveals signs of serious resistance to the process of melting from white Anglo-Americans as well as from other races. As has been suggested, a "stew pot" perhaps would be a better image toward which to aspire. In a stew, the various components complement and enhance the flavor of the whole. The absence of even one ingredient, despite its modest appearance, can detract from the richness and flavor of the entire pot. In a multicultural situation, then, the various cultures need not lose their identity in order to get along and work together for the good of all. Instead, mutual acceptance and appreciation of differences among people has the potential to generate surprising and unprecedented creativity and growth in a multicultural community, whether it be the larger civic community, the neighborhood or the church.

Since differences are difficult for many people to accept, we need to focus more on our fundamental likenesses which are all too frequently dismissed. Some of these likenesses are pointed out by Augsburger who indicates four "global constants" found among all cultures: biological similarity, psychological needs, a basic spirituality, and institutions that assist in uniting society for the common good. These universal similarities are all related to basic human needs.[11]

First, biological similarity, such as the human anatomy and its functions, crosses cultural lines, and implies that all human beings have need for proper nourishment. The mere sight of people deprived of food and water for a long period of time elicits empathy from normal people. This spontaneous reaction occurs primarily because we see that a starving person begins to lose something of the similarity to a human being. We sense a certain solidarity with other people, and we therefore react negatively to abnormal deterioration.

Second, all cultures share psychological needs—self-esteem, love, and a sense of security. In a multicultural society, marginalized people suffer most from a decline of self-esteem. Often rejected by neighbors, and lacking the presence of family and friends who live far away, persons of minority groups may feel overwhelming insecurity and loneliness.

Third, most all people share a basic spirituality that consists of something or someone transcendent, a set of moral values, and a sense of good and evil. In communities where constituents come from varied cultures, it is not uncommon to find people representing diverse religions, both Christian and non-Christian. These multicultural communities have the potential to share spiritual growth in unique and creative ways.

Fourth, "each society creates institutions that maintain the social system, unite the group by inhibiting the fracturing caused by individual self-interest, and harness the strength of persons to facilitate corporate action."[12] The need for strong community institutions that have as their major concern the welfare of all the people sometimes goes unheeded because of the fear of organizing with persons whose culture is different. However, the experience that immigrants bring with them can contribute unprecedented richness to corporate activity.

Resistance toward immigrants by American citizens

commonly stems from fear of losing jobs to people willing to work for less in order to survive. Corporations frequently take advantage of aliens who want to work, and
for the most part these people have no intention of taking
jobs away from others. But such has been the perception
of many jobless people here in the United States today. In
some cases, people's self-esteem is threatened by the
courage of immigrants who are brave enough to leave
their families, friends and familiar surroundings for an
unknown land and a strange people. Still others are victims of ignorance and prejudice.

From the perspective of immigrant people of other
cultures, there are also fears. These later arrivals in our
country sometimes resist what they experience as a con-
straint to become part of the "melting pot." They must
speak another language in order to be understood, and
their customs are often looked upon as strange. The "melting pot" image gives rise to the fear of losing their ties with
their homeland and their identity as a unique people.

Immigrants Yesterday and Today

Many well-meaning persons assume that people of
other cultures will adjust to the American way of life and
"be like the rest of us." For the most part, that was indeed
the case with European immigrants who entered this
country during the nineteenth and early twentieth centuries. Yet differences between modern immigrants and
those of the past are numerous. Timothy Matovina, focusing on the Hispanic population, suggests that the dissimi-
larities rest in six different areas.

   1. *Distance from homeland.* The ocean separated
      Europeans from their families and friends, an isola-
      tion which resulted in a forced melting pot.
      Communication was infrequent; for many pioneers,
      it was nonexistent. These circumstances left the
      immigrants no alternative but to make friends and

to "fit in." They learned the language and assimilated customs out of necessity. Contemporary Hispanic immigrants, however, have close ties with their homelands through the media, telephone and letters. These connections help reinforce language and culture.

2) *Difference in number of immigrants.* Because of the legislation of 1924, immigration was restricted. As a consequence, second generation immigrants often lacked acquaintances from their own land and therefore quickly assimilated U.S. culture and values. For Hispanics, on the other hand, the immigration flow continues. The first member of a family to arrive in this country is frequently followed by a string of relatives and friends. Language and cultural values, instead of being cast aside for new ones, are reinforced in the midst of the new culture.

3) *Poverty.* The emergence of the European immigrants from poverty to a higher standard of living enhanced assimilation into American culture. In general, the Hispanic population did not experience that rise from poverty. Through wars with Mexico (1836; 1846–1848), the U.S. annexed territory in which Mexicans who lived there had little opportunity to prosper financially. Many of these Hispanics lost their land and never rose out of poverty.

4) *Racism.* European immigrants were white and looked more like white U.S. citizens. Hispanic and African Americans, however, are notably different in skin color, a fact which often results in discrimination. Racist treatment causes a bonding with one's "own" and retards assimilation.

5) *Urbanization.* Both European and Hispanic immigrants tended to take up residence in urban areas. While European immigrants had little difficulty moving about, Hispanics and dark skinned people face greater difficulty because of poverty and racial prejudice.

6) *Church teaching on cultural adaptation.* The church's perspective on evangelization changed. In the Roman Catholic tradition, the year 1919 marked the first apostolic letter (Pope Benedict XV's *Maximum Illud*) which encouraged missionary efforts in foreign countries, but it lacked appreciation for different cultural expressions of faith. Fortunately, later church documents[13] showed a greater awareness that Catholic evangelization had often confused Western culture with values intrinsic to the gospel. *Ad Gentes* put special emphasis on adaptation of the gospel proclamation to local cultures and customs. Subsequent church documents have followed suit (i.e., *Slavorum Apostoli* [1985] and *Redemptoris Missio* [1990] by John Paul II).[14]

Cultural Transformation

Multicultural communities have the potential to stimulate a renewal and even a transformation of their members. Once we open ourselves to the differences of other cultures, we are likely to become more accepting and appreciative of our own unique selves. Self-acceptance opens the way to acceptance of other people as they are without trying to make them like ourselves. When we better understand some of the difficulties that immigrants face, we will become more empathetic to their struggles and more accepting of them as our brothers and sisters. Then their need for acceptance becomes our need for the blessings that they bring to our own faith life.

As the countenance of our country is being transformed by newcomers to our land, the movie, ET, presents us with genuine challenges. Can we accept people who are different from us, people whose color is different, whose speech is unlike ours, whose dress differs from our own, and whose customs are unfamiliar? Do we appreciate the fact that they come from another part of the world and face problems similar to those that the extraterrestrial ET encountered on coming to this planet? Obviously, the physical appearances of immigrants are more like our own than that of ET, but the treatment is all too often somewhat parallel. Reactions to unfamiliar peoples and cultures range from loving acceptance to total disregard and isolation, to psychological dissecting.

Regardless of race, color or creed, most of us live in a country which once belonged to the Native American. In that sense, nearly all of us are foreigners; we are guests in another's nation. Moreover, our own ancestral roots lie in lands far away, places which most of us have never visited. Regardless of cultural differences, Christians find their common identity in the fact that we are citizens of heaven sojourning in a world where we are all aliens.

Summary

Today our church and neighborhood communities are becoming more and more multicultural. Both the Old and New Testaments testify to God's concern for the alien. One who loves God is willing to embrace the cares and concerns of God, and to be the channels through which God's love can operate in the world.

Immigrants challenge us as Christians, and they bring a new dimension to our spiritual life. They are a continual reminder that God's Word became human out of love for us, that "he came unto his own, and his own people did not accept him" (Jn 1:11). Immigrants also challenge us to live the gospel, to see in others God incarnate among us, especially those people who are unlike us in color, culture and language. Jesus' injunction, "What you did for the least of my brothers and sisters you did for me" (Mt 25:40), sums up for people of every age the way Jesus would have us behave toward one another, especially powerless people. As we treat strangers, so we treat Jesus: "I was a stranger and you welcomed me" (Mt 25:35).

Some women feel as if they are treated as outsiders in the church. In the next chapter, we will examine the role of women in the early church, and seek to clarify any misunderstandings that may arise today from select Pauline texts.

For Further Reflection:

Gen 43:1-34
Ex 22:21-24; 23:9
The Book of Ruth
Mt 5:43-48
1 Pet 2:9-10

SUGGESTED READINGS

Brueggemann, Walter. "Welcoming the Stranger," *Interpretation and Obedience*. Fortress, 1991, pp. 290–310.

Duke, James. *Conflict and Power in Social Life*. Brigham Young University Press, 1976.

Elliott, J. H. *Home for the Homeless*. SCM Press, 1981.

Fitzpatrick, Joseph P., S.J., *One Church, Many Cultures*. Sheed & Ward, 1987.

Freire, Paulo. *Cultural Action for Freedom*. Harvard University Press, 1970.

Gittins, Anthony J. *Gifts and Strangers: Meeting the Challenge of Inculturation*. Paulist, 1989.

Gowan, Donald G. "Wealth and Poverty in the Old Testament: The Care of the Widows, the Orphan, and the Sojourner," *Interpretation* 41 (1987) 341–353.

Ignatieff, Michael. *The Needs of Strangers*. Viking, 1985.

Lang, Bernard. "The Social Organization of Peasant Poverty in Biblical Israel," *Journal for the Study of the Old Testament* 24 (1982) 47-63.

Mainelli, Helen Koenig. "Aliens in Our Midst," *The Bible Today* (July, 1991) 204-207.

Newmark, Eileen. *Women's Roles: A Cross-Cultural Perspective.* Pergamon Press, 1980.

Ogletree, Thomas W. *Hospitality to the Stranger: Dimensions of Moral Understanding.* Fortress, 1985.

Schineller, Peter, S.J. *A Handbook of Inculturation.* Paulist, 1989.

Westermann, Claus. *Genesis 12-36.* Trans. by John Scullion. Augsburg, 1985.

5

Embracing the Church Feminine

*In Christ Jesus you are all children of God
through faith.... There is neither male nor female,
for you are all one in Christ Jesus (Gal 3:26–28).*

A spirituality that is both scriptural and ecclesial embraces feminine as well as masculine gifts in the church. We have no better paradigm for recognition of the feminine gifts in the church than the early post-resurrection church itself. The gospels attest to the fact that women played important roles in Jesus' life during his ministry and his passion as well as after his resurrection. Although Jesus died much earlier, the gospels (thought to have been written between A.D. 70 and 100) nevertheless reflect the teachings, attitudes, and activities of the historical Jesus.

Mary, Model Disciple

Although there is little written about Mary in the gospels, this young woman from Nazareth stands out as a person of deep faith and unwavering courage. She dared to believe that God could do great things, even the impossible. Mary knew that the Hebrew scriptures of her people carried story after story of God's intervention on their behalf. It mattered not that she was a woman of humble origins; the nomadic and unlettered Abraham and Sarah were proof that God had a preference for the simple folk. For Mary, then, it was not difficult to believe that God could "lift up the lowly" (Lk 1:52). She had great expectations of God, and her faith convinced her that nothing was impossible. God could bring about a reversal of long established injustices that had left poor people hungry (Lk 1:46–55). She was a woman who dared to dream big dreams for her people.

The early church remembered Mary as a model for all disciples.[1] She did not claim rank based on her role as the physical mother of God. Rather, from what we know of the testimony of her son in the gospel, her significance lay in listening to what God wanted of her and acting accordingly:

> And he [Jesus] was told, "Your mother and your brothers are standing outside, desiring to see you." But he said to them, "My mother and my brothers are those who hear the word of God and do it" (Lk 8:20–21).

Already in the infancy narrative of Luke's gospel, Mary had demonstrated her radical obedience to God's word spoken to her through the angel.

Jesus' saying that "whoever loses one's life for my sake will save it" (Lk 9:24) also finds its paradigm of courage in Mary at the annunciation:

> Behold, I am the handmaid of the Lord; let it be done to me according to your word (Lk 1:38; RSV).

In view of first-century Jewish culture, this unwed, pregnant Jewish woman's response demonstrates untold faith and courage. According to Jewish law, an unmarried woman found to be pregnant was subject to death by stoning. Yet the danger Mary faced did not modify her faith-filled reply. For that reason, throughout the centuries, Mary has been a model for people who would risk their lives in service of God's people. This woman of trust, faith, and courage set the example for her son. Later, in Gethsemani, Jesus faced the fears of death with submission to God's will with words similar to those of his mother on the occasion of the annunciation of his birth: "Not my will but yours be done" (Lk 22:42).

The early church recognized Mary's obedience to God in another difficult situation. For example, Matthew tells us that Herod attempted to kill the infant Jesus. Along with Joseph and her infant son, Mary had to flee to the far-off country of Egypt and live there as an alien in order to save her child's life (Mt 2:13–15). Like an ideal disciple, she was willing to take risks. She left her family, her familiar surroundings, and her Jewish culture for the sake of Jesus. Whatever had to be done, Mary simply did it.

Mary was also remembered as a woman sensitive to the needs of others. At a wedding feast in the town of Cana, it was "the mother of Jesus" who told her son what had gone amiss: "They have no wine" (Jn 2:3). When Jesus seemed to take the matter rather lightly, she simply told the waiters to do whatever Jesus told them (Jn 2:5).

Throughout the gospel of John, "the mother of Jesus" is never named, because the writer did not want to limit her motherhood. Jesus designated her as the mother of the Beloved Disciple and the Beloved Disciple as her son. By that characterization, Jesus identified his mother as the paradigm out of which all discipleship is born and upon which it is modeled. In the Jewish world of Jesus' day, a person was identified in terms of family, clan or tribe.[2] Their actions were thus judged according to their origins—like mother, like son or daughter. For that reason, Jesus identified his opponents in the gospel of John as belonging to the family of Satan. Their lies would lead to the death of Jesus:

> You are of your father the devil, and your will is to do your father's desires. He was a murderer from the beginning, and has nothing to do with the truth, because there is no truth in him. When he lies, he speaks according to his own nature, for he is a liar and the father of lies.... The one who is of God hears the words of God;

the reason you do not hear them is that you are
not of God (Jn 8:44–47).

Like the mother of Jesus, the Beloved Disciple, who
stayed with Jesus throughout his sufferings and death on
the cross, is never named in the gospel of John. Perhaps
the author wanted the reader to see in that disciple, not
an individual person, but a way of life to be imitated.
Just as that disciple was entrusted to the mother of Jesus
(Jn 19:26–27), so likewise every disciple who belongs to
the family of Jesus is entrusted to her. Henceforth, the
mother of Jesus would nurture obedience to God in all
future disciples as she did in those who would have good
wine at the wedding feast of Cana: "Do whatever he tells
you" (Jn 2:15).

Those are Mary's words to us today. In the pages of
the gospels, Mary continues as a model for us. Just as she
took her place at the foot of the cross, so also will she
accompany us in our following of Jesus. Should we have
to drink the "bitter wine" as did her son,[3] we can count
on her to be there with us to the end.

Jesus and Women

Women's gifts in the early church are especially high-
lighted in the writings of Luke. Women are characterized
as persons in whom God found fertile ground for surprising activity. Elizabeth and Anna are portrayed as older
women who knew how to receive gifts from God without
complaints about bad timing for these astonishing surprises (Lk 1:25, 38).[4] There was no murmuring from
Elizabeth to the effect that she was now too old to care for
a child, or questions about why God didn't think about
this a little sooner. She understood her pregnancy as a
direct act of mercy on her from the one to whom age was
no impediment for the accomplishment of great things.

Anna, a widowed prophetess in her eighties, was an
active evangelizer in the temple. Luke tells us that as

soon as she saw Jesus, "She gave thanks to God, and spoke of him to all who were looking for the redemption of Jerusalem" (Lk 2:38; RSV).

Women in the gospels do not seem to be inhibited by social customs. Just because women hadn't done it before was no reason they should not follow their rabbi, Jesus. The phenomenon of women following a teacher was an unconventional and innovative occurrence in first-century Palestine.[5] Yet Jesus did not hesitate to deviate from conventions that restricted his mission of spreading the good news of God's reign. According to the writings of the New Testament, therefore, women together with men played an important role in spreading the gospel message in the early Christian movement.

An unnamed woman in the gospel breaks all kinds of first-century social mores. She, too, saw what needed to be done and did it. Jesus was dining at the home of one of the Pharisees. No one showed Jesus any special courtesy by washing his feet when he arrived, as was done to honored guests in that culture. So a woman bathed his feet in her own tears and wiped them dry with her hair. What Simon should have provided but ignored, this woman contributed out of the poverty of her own being (Lk 7:36–50).

The first two gospels tell us about a Gentile woman and mother who had her priorities in order. Her little girl was possessed with an evil spirit; that was reason enough in the mind of this woman to risk anything. She went to Jesus and begged him to cast out the demon. Jesus seemed to have a problem with that, but the woman would not be so easily deterred, not even by the arrogance of his disciples who begged him to get rid of her. This Syrophoenician woman coaxed Jesus not to limit his ministry to his own people. She challenged him to extend his healing powers beyond the boundaries of the Jewish people to a little Gentile girl. Not only did Jesus grant her request, but he also praised her for her faith (Mk 7:24–30; Mt 15:21–28).

All the gospels affirm that women accompanied Jesus in Palestine, that they went with him from Galilee up to Jerusalem, and that they were present at his death:

> There were also women looking on from afar, among whom were Mary Magdalene, and Mary the mother of James the younger and of Joses, and Salome, who, when he was in Galilee, followed him, and ministered to him; and also many other women who came up with him to Jerusalem (Mk 15:40-41; see also Mt 27:55-56; Lk 23:49; Jn 19:25-27; RSV).

With no mention of men at the tomb, Matthew, Mark and Luke affirm the presence of women when the stone was rolled over the tomb after the crucifixion (Mt 27:61; Mk 15:47; Lk 23:55). All the gospels mention that women were the first to arrive at the empty tomb on that first Easter morning.

Women in John's gospel encounter Jesus and believe in him simply on the basis of their experience rather than on the witness of some important figure. For example, the woman whom Jesus met at the well in Samaria was the first to proclaim to the Samaritan people the good news that Jesus was the messiah. In her conversation with Jesus, she teased out his identity based on the knowledge she had of her own religious traditions. Once convinced that Jesus could be the long awaited messiah, she went into the city and told the people. "Many Samaritans from that city believed in him because of the woman's testimony" (Jn 4:39). This unlearned village woman from Samaria had listened and understood Jesus.

In contrast, Nicodemus, the learned rabbi from Jerusalem in John's gospel, could not grasp the meaning of Jesus' words. Surely anyone who could work the signs Jesus did must be from God, he reasoned. But when Jesus began to talk about being reborn of water and the Spirit, Nicodemus couldn't figure that out. How could one be born again (Jn 3:1–14)? Nicodemus thought in terms of logic, but logic got in his way, because God doesn't always work from a logical agenda.

The gospel of John gives us still another woman who didn't need the witness of others to believe. Mary Magdalene was the first to go forth with the good news, "I have seen the Lord" (Jn 20:18). In her ardent love for Jesus, she had risen early "while it was still dark" and hurried to the tomb on the first day of the week after Jesus' death. On finding it empty, she ran to tell Peter and the other disciple. These two disciples ran to the tomb, and on finding it to be as Mary Magdalene had said, they returned home. Mary Magdalene, however, stayed there weeping in sorrow despite the danger of associating herself with a crucified criminal. Jesus appeared to her before appearing to any of the disciples. At first, Mary Magdalene thought he was the gardener: "Sir, if you have carried him away, tell me where you have laid him, and I will take him away" (Jn 20:13). She was not concerned about how she would carry the dead weight of the body, nor was she worried about what the Roman soldiers might do. As a woman who loved deeply, anything was possible. She simply knew in her heart what had to be done if only she could retrieve the body. Just how she would do it would have to be worked out in the process. We can only imagine the stirrings in both of their hearts when Jesus simply uttered her name, "Mary" (Jn 20:16).

Women in the Pauline Writings

Later, women played a major role in Paul's missionary work. Since the Pauline letters are the oldest writings in the New Testament, some people point an accusing finger at Paul as the primary person responsible for the lack of appreciation of women in the church. However, that picture is not consistent with the general tone of the authentic letters of Paul. In his letter to the Galatians, for example, he speaks of the unity and equality of all persons in Christ:

There is neither Jew nor Greek, there is neither slave nor free, there is neither male nor female; for you are all one in Christ Jesus (Gal 3:28).

In order to emphasize the importance of each member in the church community, Paul uses the human body in a striking analogy. Just as each part of the human body needs the others in order to function well, so it is with the church:

> For just as the body is one and has many members, and all the members of the body, though many, are one body, so it is with Christ. For by one Spirit we were all baptized into one body.... For the body does not consist in one member but of many. If the foot should say, "Because I am not an eye, I do not belong to the body," that would not make it any less a part of the body. If the whole body were an eye, where would be the hearing? If the whole body were an ear, where would be the sense of smell? But as it is God arranged the organs in the body, each one of them, as he chose. If all were a single organ, where would the body be? As it is, there are many parts, yet one body. The eye cannot say to the hand, "I have no need of you," nor again the head to the feet, "I have no need of you".... If one member suffers, all suffer together; if one member is honored, all rejoice together. Now you are the body of Christ and individually members of it (1 Cor 12:12–27).

Women bring unique gifts to the church's apostolic mission. This fact has been verified in parishes where women and men work together in team ministry. The positive results of collaboration between men and women in pastoral life highlight all the more how the exclusion of women from approved roles in the church limits the effectiveness of the church as a whole. Each person is important and plays a crucial part in building up "the body of Christ."

In his letter to the Roman church community, written some twenty years after the death and resurrection of Jesus, Paul commends and supports the work of women in the church. He sends the following recommendation regarding a woman by the name of Phoebe:

> I commend to you our sister Phoebe, a deaconess of the church at Cenchreae, that you may receive her in the Lord as befits the saints, and help her in whatever she may require from you, for she has been a helper of many and of myself as well (Rom 16:1).

Without doubt, Phoebe was a leader whom Paul valued in the church at Cenchreae.[6] Moreover, she obviously had assisted Paul as well as many community members in other church houses.

Paul refers to the bravery of a certain woman and man, Prisca and Aquila, who were deeply involved in the early Christian movement. They are remembered by Paul in his letter to the Roman Christian community as having taken great risks in assisting him:

> Greet Prisca and Aquilla, my co-workers in Christ Jesus, who risked their necks for my life, to whom not only I but also all the churches of the Gentiles give thanks; greet also the church in their house (Rom 16:3–5).

Paul's letters, together with Luke's account of Paul's activity in the early church in the Acts of the Apostles, give one firm reason to believe that anyone who assisted Paul in his missionary work must have done so at great risk. The fact that Prisca and Aquilla used their house as a gathering place for local Christians could have caused suspicion about their activities. The ways of the Christians were mysterious to outsiders. Their refusal to join social groups connected with various religious cults and their celebration of the Lord's supper made them look strange. Nevertheless, danger did not deter Prisca and Aquilla from their cooperative ministry in the church.

Paul also greets Andronicus and Junia (or Junias) in the letter to the Romans as persons who had shared prison with him (Rom 16:7). The Greek form of the name "Junias," *Iounian*, could be masculine or feminine in the form in which it is used. Since some ancient manuscripts of Paul's letters support the feminine form,[7] Junia and Andronicus are thought by many biblical scholars to be a married couple who had been imprisoned with Paul.

Certainly Christian women were more active in their churches than were their contemporaries within Judaism.[8] Undoubtedly, this digression from Jewish culture began with Jesus himself.

Women in the Post-Pauline Writings

There are certain passages in the New Testament which are often used to justify subordination of women to men. They are also utilized in the effort to deny women the use of their talents in service of the church. The most frequently quoted citation appears in the first letter to Timothy:

> Let a woman learn in silence with all submissiveness. I permit no women to teach or to have authority over men; she is to keep silent. For Adam was formed first, then Eve; and Adam was not deceived, but the woman was deceived and became a transgressor. Yet woman will be saved through bearing children, if she continues in faith and love and holiness, with modesty (1 Tim 2:11–15; RSV).

This letter opens with a greeting in which Paul appears to be the author. The letter begins: "Paul, an apostle of Christ Jesus by command of God our Savior and of Christ Jesus our hope, to Timothy, my true child in faith (1 Tim 1:1). Most biblical scholars agree, however, that the pastoral letters (1 and 2 Timothy and Titus) were not written by St. Paul. The reference to already existing church structures or offices indicate that they reflect a period later than that which is reflected in the authentic Pauline letters of the 50's A.D.

These pastoral letters, bearing the name of Paul as their author, are thought to have been written around A.D. 100–110 long after Paul's martyrdom.[9] In no way were they meant to deceive the pastors to whom they were addressed. The use of pseudonyms in such documents was common in the Graeco-Roman philosophical tradition. The authors followed that tradition and set forth a teaching that was presumed would be the mind of Paul were he still alive at that time.

The pastoral letters were attempts to address particular critical situations and times in early church history. The late first century was the period in which Christianity was forced to become a religion separate from Judaism. At that time, the empire was hostile to strange religious sects which were not officially recognized. When Paul wrote his letters, Christians were considered Jews; they were still a part of regular Jewish worship both in the temple and in the synagogues. Judaism was an established and acceptable religion in the Roman Empire, and Christianity had hovered under the same protective umbrella. Around A.D. 85, however, it became obvious that the religious beliefs of the two groups could not be reconciled. Christianity was forced out of Jewish institutions mostly because of their insistence on the messiahship and divinity of Jesus Christ. Once the rift between Jews and Jewish Christians widened and clashes ensued, Christianity had to become a religion independent of Judaism and had to survive on its own. The pastoral letters were written during this crisis.

Some scholars maintain that in order to become a religion respected by the empire, some Christians believed it was necessary to "pull in the reins" on women and have them behave as women were expected to act in the Graeco-Roman culture and particularly in Judaism.[10] Men would take up the leadership of the church, and women would fade into the background and thereby eliminate an external distinction that set Christianity apart. Such a move seemed necessary, it was believed, for the survival of the fledgling community. The more Christianity resembled Judaism in the eyes of the imperial leaders, the greater chance it had to survive.

Sociological studies indicate that the hierarchy of persons in the church community which is reflected in the pastoral letters is consistent with the household codes in existence at that time in the Roman Empire.[11] The father was the head of the household, the mother under him, and so on down to the slaves. The late first-century church patterned the church community on this code of order so as to project itself as a disciplined organization that would enhance order in the empire, rather than one that would threaten the established order. Thus, the freedom and equality which women had enjoyed in following Jesus and which carried over into the early post-resurrection church of Paul's time began to disappear.

How do we account for the passage in the first letter to the Corinthians concerning the subordination of women? All scholars agree that this is an authentic letter of Paul. The following passage is frequently cited as a basis for the exclusion of women from apostolic activity in the church:

> As in the churches of all the saints, the women should keep silence in the churches. For they are not permitted to speak, but should be subordinate, as even the law says. If there is anything they desire to know, let them ask their hus-

> bands at home. For it is shameful for a woman
> to speak in church (1 Cor 14:34-35).

These verses deal with discipline to be observed by women in the church assembly. However, the subject matter of the chapter is spiritual gifts, especially prophecy and speaking in tongues. Verses 34 and 35, scholars have noted, appear to deviate from the subject and disrupt the flow of the reading. If these verses are omitted, the chapter reads smoothly without the interruption. Hence, some contemporary scholars maintain that the passage was inserted at a later date before the closing of the canon, probably about the time of the letter to Timothy.[12] The insertion of the text, according to scholarly opinion, may have been made by a scribe or church leader/s who wished to reflect the late first-century restriction on women's active participation in church ministry. "If Paul were here today," they might have reasoned, "he would make the changes in customs that are necessary for the church to survive." While the struggle for survival has long since ceased, the involvement of women in the church is still viewed with suspicion by many people.

Another passage that is often used in attempts to verify a scriptural basis for inequality of women and men comes from the letter to the Ephesians. It insists on maintaining a hierarchy of persons in the "household" of the church:

> Wives be subject to your husbands as to the
> Lord. For the husband is the head of the wife as
> Christ is the head of the church, his body, and is
> himself its Savior (Eph 5:22).

This passage is located in the context of a code of conduct for the household of God. The citation presents Christ's love for the church as the model for a husband's love for his wife. The order required is based on the imperial household codes of the late first century, the purpose of which were to establish hierarchically ordered social units and thus contribute to the order of society. Late first-century Christianity may have adopted this household model in response to accusations that the Christians were disruptive and threatened the "social fabric by advocating equality among its adherents."[13]

The structure of the Graeco-Roman world was decidedly patriarchal, and it permeated all the political, religious and social institutions of the empire. Even though early Christianity struck deep at the roots of the system in its vision of the dignity and equality of all persons, nevertheless near the end of the first century, there was compromise with the social mores of the day. Donald Senior makes the following observation:

> There should be no scandal in this. Vatican II's Dogmatic Constitution on Divine Revelation reminds us that the New Testament is not a bloodless charter of ideals dropped untouched from heaven. It is a text that exudes genuine human experience as the Spirit of God works and groans within the realities of history. So the Scriptures are not only the touchpoint for our ideals but we can also locate there the evidence of our failures.[14]

Women in the Contemporary Church

Passages such as 1 Corinthians 14:34–35 and 1 Timothy 2:11–15 cannot be used as a biblical basis for rejection of women's participation in the contemporary church's apostolic mission. Women in the Roman Catholic Church today, while not admitted to ordained ministry, are officially allowed to function in many other roles common to lay people (i.e., Vicars for Religious, Ministers of the Eucharist). Yet in spite of the church's teaching at Vatican II, which emphasized the need for participation by the laity, many people are still opposed to allowing women to exercise any ministerial role in the church, even those which the church has approved. Frequently, this resistance comes from uninformed persons who think that church rules are being violated. Pope John Paul II, no doubt aware of opposition regarding women's participation in the mission of the church, reiterated the conciliar mandate of 1965 with a quote from the Decree on the Apostolate of the Laity:

> Since in our days women are taking an increasingly active share in the whole of society, it is very important that they participate more widely also in the various fields of the church's apostolate (*Apostolicam Actuositatem, 9*).[15]

The Pope again stressed the need to recognize the equality of man and woman:

> Making reference to Pope John XXIII, who saw women's greater consciousness of their proper dignity and their entrance into public life as signs of our times, the Synod Fathers, when confronted with the various forms of discrimination and marginization to which women are subjected simply because they are women, time and time again strongly affirmed the urgency to defend and to promote the personal dignity of woman, and consequently, her equality with man.... Only through openly acknowledging the personal dignity of women is the first step taken to promote the full participation of women in Church life as well as in social and public life.[16]

In spite of the church's promotion of women's roles in our contemporary church, negative attitudes toward ministry by women still prevail. The two major causes appear to be culture and a concentration on certain biblical passages that have been badly misinterpreted. Studies show that cultural discrimination as well as religious biases toward women exist not only in the United States but throughout the world:

> The overwhelming evidence of anthropological studies of male and female roles is that virtually no society in the world offers women equal status with men.[17].

Even though there has been progress over the last decade, our Western culture tolerates with varying degrees the same discrimination toward women that most other cultures do. In the labor world, for example, women are often expected to take certain roles which are considered feminine. When that expectation is disregarded, women sometimes have to prove themselves by enduring situations from which men are exempted in the same area of work. In the political arena, women are often subjected to scrutinies from which men in the same contest are excused.

Discrimination within the church takes various forms. Roles that women are allowed to exercise are sometimes given to men who are less qualified. Frequently, the mistaken notion that "men have always done that work in the church" poses the obstacle. At times, discrimination comes from the failure to accept the essential equality of men and women. Pope John Paul II, however, reminds Catholics that the equality of men and women "constitutes the most obvious basis for the dignity and vocation of women in the Church and in the world" (*Mulieres Dignitatem 16*).

Custom or Doctrine?

Biblical evidence in both Old and New Testaments provides us with a picture of God's people who changed and modified customs and rules of discipline as they faced new challenges and needs. In the Old Testament,

Saul and David move the people from a failing tribal organization to a monarchy in order to meet the threats of surrounding nations. Later, the monarchy failed, and by the time of Jesus, the process of Hellenization under the Greeks divided the people of God into factions (i.e., Pharisees, Sadducees, etc.) with whom Jesus clashed. He wouldn't abide by some of their customs which heaped needless burdens upon the people. With the death of Jesus came other changes, especially the question of carrying the message not only to Jews but to Gentiles as well. "Thus biblical peoples derived their language, their culture, their political structure, and even much of their theology from their surrounding environment."[18]

The original suppression the role of women in the church's apostolic mission occurred because of situations that no longer exist. Just as change in custom was brought about because of need at that time, so also the church continues to change past customs, not doctrine, in order to meet contemporary needs. In its attempt to respond to the needs of God's people today, the flexibility of the early church as presented in the New Testament provides much wisdom.

With the assistance of advanced biblical scholarship and its vision of the church as "the people of God," Vatican Council II (1961–65) stressed the dignity and equality of all people, a dignity and equality "that arises from baptism in Christ."[19] Women are not to be viewed as less honorable than men, and along with men, they are to be active in the church's mission.

The resilience of the church with regard to previous practices springs from the church's belief and recognition of the Holy Spirit's ongoing work and presence in the church:

The Spirit of truth will guide you into all the truth...and will declare to you the things that are to come" (John 16:13).

Despite the fact that more areas of service in the church are now open to women than twenty-five years ago, the church's ministry still suffers. Progress and changes that need to be made are frequently rejected, or they come about too slowly.

Women, with their unique talents and characteristics, are indispensable to the growth of the church. The church as the body of Christ envisioned by Paul needs every member in order to effectively proclaim the good news of Jesus Christ.

Summary

Cultural and religious traditions have long been the major sources to which many people have clung in their efforts to keep women within the bounds of assigned feminine roles. Sacred scripture has often been misinterpreted and misused in efforts to diminish the role of women in the church.

Erroneous interpretation of the letters of Paul has been the principal basis of much oppression of women both within the church and in society. However, a correct understanding of passages often cited from these writings depends on sound sociological studies of the culture and time out of which these writings emerged. Such studies reveal a Paul quite different from the often quoted so-called "woman-hater." Moreover, scholarly investigations have demonstrated that most of the frequently cited passages used to keep women "in their place" come from a post-Pauline church. The infant church of the late first and early second century was struggling for survival under various types of persecution in the Roman Empire. The freedom and equality that women appear to have enjoyed in the first decades of the early church were curtailed as a measure of defense against exterior forces of annihilation.

According to some scholars, these restrictions were enjoined on the church for cultural reasons in order to appear less conspicuous in an empire hostile to Christianity. Since the activities of women in the church may have been perceived as bizarre by outsiders, the progress of the church and even it's very survival may have been the deciding factors involved.

Today, however, the church no longer suffers the threat of extinction because of women's activities. Vatican II encouraged active and responsible lay participation in the church without distinction between men and women. Many times in the history of the church, the ecclesial structures themselves permitted and encouraged women in leadership roles. Abbesses and women superiors of religious orders exercised great influence in the church. Sts. Catherine of Siena and Teresa of Avila left a distinctive mark on the church of their day. Women have special gifts to offer the church; without them both the church and society are impoverished.

The declining years of our lives bring a certain leveling to both women and men of all social strata. In the following chapter, we will examine "aging" as a time of growing closer to God and others.

For Further Reflection:

Jn 4:1–42
Jn 20:1–31
1 Cor 12:4–30
Rom 16:1–16

SUGGESTED READINGS

Haughton, Rosemary. *The Recreation of Eve.* Templegate, 1985.
Johnson, Elizabeth A. "A Modern Mary," *Praying* 5:4 (May-June, 1993) 4–8.
Johnson, Luke Timothy. "Luke 24:1–11," *Interpretation* 46:1 (Jan. 1992) 57–61.

Maloney, Francis J. *Women First among the Faithful.* Ave Maria, 1986.

"Partners in the Mystery of Redemption. A Pastoral Response to Women's Concerns for Church and Society," *Origins* 17:45 (April 21, 1988).

Resseguie, J. L. "Making the Familiar Seem Strange: Luke 7:36–50," *Interpretation* 46:3 (July, 1992) 285–290.

Senior, Donald. "Roles of Women in Scripture: A Perspective from the Church's Universal Mission," *Women in the Church* I. Ed. Madonna Kolbenschlag. The Pastoral Press, 1987, 3–17.

Stambaugh, John E., and David Balch, *The New Testament and Its Social Environment.* Westminster, 1983.

Verner, D. C. *The Household of God: The Social World of the Pastoral Epistles.* Scholars Press, 1983.

6

Growing Older

In old age they still produce fruit;
they are always green and full of sap (Ps 92:14).

The title of this chapter is meant to emphasize "grow-ing" in contrast to simply "becoming" older by reason of the laws of nature. "Growing" older implies for this author that a person embraces the aging process with faith. Therefore, we will examine from a faith point of view some of the issues related to aging in oneself and in others, especially family members.

Journey toward Wholeness

A spirituality rooted in scripture embraces every stage of life. As Christians, we know that God's creative power is continuously at work in us throughout our lives, for St. Paul assures us, "God is at work in you, both to will and to work for God's good pleasure" (Phil 2:14). Thus our entire life-span can be perceived not only as a journey in compa-ny with God who eagerly awaits our coming home (2 Cor 5:8; Phil 1:23), but also as a journey that is enlivened and sparked by the very life of Christ himself. The promise Jesus made to the Samaritan woman at the well is a promise fulfilled in us at Baptism and gradually brought to perfect integration throughout the course of life:

> The water that I will give will become in them a
> spring of water gushing up to eternal life (Jn
> 4:14).

Awareness of Christ's intimate presence during the whole of our life-journey gives our lives a spark that can-not be quenched by any external power. St. Paul knew that presence and, without doubt, it was that awareness that sustained him through his long journeys and tribulations:

> If God is for us, who is against us? He who did not spare his own Son but gave him up for us all, will he not also give us all things with him?... Who will separate us from the love of Christ? Will hardship, or distress, or persecution, or famine, or nakedness, or peril, or sword?...In all these things we are more than conquerors through him who loved us. For I am convinced that neither death, nor life, nor angels, nor rulers, nor things present, nor things to come, nor powers, nor height, nor depth, nor anything else in all creation, will be able to separate us from the love of God in Christ Jesus our Lord (Rom 8:31-39; RSV).

Suffering and Aging

Although every one of us is aging, there is a pervasive denial of that process in American society. Television ads entice us to search for the fountain of youth. There is a mania for looking young which gives the impression that there is something wrong with looking old. Yet growth toward maturity is an experience universal to all of creation. For human beings, the process of aging began the moment we were born. Although the humor that accompanies fortieth birthdays provides a lot of good healthy laughs, such quips as being "over the hill" reflect an attitude common to a great percentage of people in our North American culture.

Our Western society tends to categorize people according to three stages: childhood, adulthood and old age. Life is not viewed as a continuous process. Childhood is frequently looked upon as a period of dependence, energy and playfulness; adulthood is generally perceived as the stage of productivity, independence and vigorous life. Old age, on the other hand, is often viewed negatively as a second childhood, a time of physical and mental weakness. Miriam Corcoran's poem challenges society's preference for the early stages of life:

Aging and Ageism

Woman of the Whole Year
Have you ever known a woman named "November"?
Neither have I.
Now "May" and "June and "April" have their
  namesakes—
Ever ask why?

We rarely picture woman as autumnal;
Female is spring.
Please, someone, name a newborn girl "October"
And hear her sing

Of harvest cut and growth complete and fruit
  mature,
Not just of birth.
Oh, let a woman age as seasons do;
Love each time's worth![1]

The aging process is often feared because of the signs of physical deterioration. In the following passage from *Ecclesiastes*, Qoheleth poetically expresses his fears concerning the declining years. He describes old age in terms of physical difficulties, as a time when the winter of life, unlike the seasonal winter, gives way to spring only at death. The picture is one with which many people can identify:

Remember your Creator while you are still young,
  before the bad days come,
  before the years come which, you will say, give you
    no pleasure;
  before the sun and the light grow dim

and the moon and stars,
before the clouds return after the rain;
the time when your watchmen become shaky,
when strong men are bent double,
when the women, one by one, quit grinding,
and, as they look out of the window, find their sight
    growing dim.
When the street-door is kept shut,
when the sound of grinding fades away,
when the first cry of a bird wakes you up,
when all the singing has stopped;
when going uphill is an ordeal
and you are frightened at every step you take...
while you are on your way to your everlasting home
and the mourners are assembling in the street...
the dust returns to the earth from which it came,
and the spirit returns to God who gave it (Eccl 12:1-7;
NJB).

As a faith people, however, we might look upon our own bodily degeneration, as well as that of our loved ones, as a visible reminder that day by day we are approaching our goal in this life, be it imminent or perhaps delayed for years. This is not to deny that sickness and frailty most often accompany the more advanced stages of aging; rather, it is a means of encountering life's hardships with a faith that gives meaning even to suffering.

Looking at suffering in the light of scripture can enable us not only to endure the inevitable, but also to grow in holiness during moments when we are physically weak. St. Paul provides a good example. He considered his afflictions as indications that whatever he accomplished in his ministry was through the power of God and not through his own strength:

We have this treasure in clay jars, so that it may
be made clear that this extraordinary power

belongs to God and does not come from us (2 Cor 4:7).

Paul also looked upon his suffering as a manifestation of the life and sufferings of Jesus in his body:

> We are...always carrying in the body the death of Jesus, so that the life of Jesus may also be made visible in our bodies (2 Cor 4:8–10).

Paul aimed his vision beyond the present; he spoke of his suffering as a gradual physical degeneration that was giving way to inner newness. He considered his sufferings not as an isolated aspect of life, but in context and together with the glory that would be his in the future. For that reason, even though his afflictions in themselves seemed to be overwhelming (2 Cor 1:8), he could speak of them as being slight (2 Cor 4:17) when compared to the glory to which they would give way. In fact, Paul viewed these sufferings as a preparation for receiving future glory:

> Even though our outer nature is wasting away, our inner nature is being renewed day by day. For this slight momentary affliction is preparing us for an eternal weight of glory beyond all measure....for what can be seen is temporary, but what cannot be seen is eternal (2 Cor 4:16–17).

By the "outer nature," the apostle is referring to earthly existence. The "inner nature" is that which strives toward the new creation "through daily renewal by the Spirit."[2] The signs of old age speak not only of death but especially of eternal life because, as St. Paul asserts, the one who raised Jesus from the dead will also raise us from death to new life (2 Cor 4:14).

Envisioning the Goal

Beginning in the last decade, there has been much talk about quality of life for the aged. Many times quality of life, however, is judged from the viewpoint of physical health alone. If a person lacks physical well-being, then some people maintain that the person in question is bereft of quality of life and hence should be helped to end life. Unquestionably, advanced maturity is often accompanied by debilitating diseases. Nevertheless, poor health does not mean that life has to be without purpose or meaning. Countless senior citizens continue to experience happiness and accomplishments in their advanced years even though many of them have serious health problems.

Failing health and ill-fortune certainly did not rob Paul of quality of life. The letter to the Philippians is thought to be one of the last letters Paul wrote before he died. He was an old man, tired and imprisoned, but this letter surpasses those of his younger days in tenderness, eloquence, and theological insight. He ponders the meaning of life, suffering and death as he pens the missive to the Philippian community.

> I want you to know, beloved, that what has happened to me actually helped to spread the gospel, so that it has become known throughout the whole imperial guard and to everyone else that my imprisonment is for Christ (Phil 1:12–13).

Paul has his eye on the goal, not looking back but looking forward:

> [This] one thing I do: forgetting what lies behind and straining forward to what lies ahead, I press on toward the goal for the prize of the heavenly call of God in Christ Jesus (Phil 3:13–14).

If we keep our eyes on the goal as Paul did, our sufferings can be compared to the pruning process. Once the tree blossoms, we soon forget how barren it looked at the time of pruning.

Frequently men and women who have reached old age must walk this unfamiliar path alone. When elderly persons speak of impending death, family members or friends often respond with remarks of denial: "Oh, you'll live to be a hundred years old." Sharon Curtin speaks of the tragedy of such denial:

> Avoiding looking at the entire life cycle, pretending that death doesn't exist, or is somehow in bad taste, robs the old of the chance to complete their life. It denies that death has any meaning, that there is any knowledge or experience to be gained in dying as well as in living, and leaves only a sense of despair.[3]

When family and friends of an aged loved one negate his or her later life experience, they miss a grace-filled opportunity not only to walk the last mile with the person, but also to reflect on its meaning for their own lives.

Since our society places so much value on productivity and fails to recognize the worth of the person, many of the aged suffer identity crises. Once they were esteemed as significant persons, only to find themselves in later years left aside and replaced by the younger generation. A great number of them have been parents with children who in years past looked to them for guidance. Now, in their declining condition, they become dependent on those same children. Others have been distinguished citizens, held important positions at work, and were respected as intelligent and creative persons. As retirees, they find that many people look upon them as being less important and less useful.

The inherent dignity of the Christian, however, is not tied to productivity. Regardless of age or physical condition, one's status of belonging to the family of God cannot be affected by society's standards for the value of a person. A Christian's identity is that of a daughter or son of a loving God and a brother or sister of Jesus (Rom 8:15–17). From a faith point of view, nothing can annihilate or supersede this familial relationship with God.

Paul experienced loneliness and deprivation as do many older people today. Like many aging parents, he chides the Philippians, while at the same time he makes excuses for their neglect of him:

> I rejoice in the Lord greatly that now at last you have revived your concern for me; indeed, you were concerned for me, but had no opportunity to show it. Not that I am referring to being in need; for I have learned to be content with whatever I have. I know what it is to have little, and I know what it is to have plenty. In any and all circumstances I have learned the secret of being well-fed and of going hungry, of having plenty and of being in need. I can do all things through him who strengthens me. In any case, it was kind of you to share my distress (Phil 4:10–14).

Obviously, Paul never denied his loneliness and sufferings. When he wrote to the Corinthians with whom he had spent much time, he says:

> We are afflicted in every way but not crushed; perplexed but not driven to despair; persecuted but not forsaken; struck down but not destroyed (2 Cor 4:8–9).

However, Paul did not dwell on his sufferings in a narcissistic manner. Keeping his eye on the goal, he saw them as temporary afflictions that would be followed by eternal glory (2 Cor 4:16–18). He also considered suffering as an opportunity to suffer with Christ:

For his sake I have suffered the loss of all things
in order that I may gain Christ... that I may
know him and the power of his resurrection
and may share his sufferings (Phil 3:8–10; also
see Rom 8:17-18; RSV).

Companioning the Elderly

The depths of a person's spirituality is reflected in
the respect and love shown to every person regardless of
age, health or social status. Isaiah judged the decadence
of Israelite society on the attitude of the people toward
the elderly:

[The] youth will be insolent to the elder, and the
base to the honorable (Is 3:5b).[4]

In order to become spiritually mature persons, we need
our older friends and relatives as much as they need us.
As we observe those who once were powerful persons
becoming dependent, and the strong growing weak, they
become living reminders to us of what is really important in life. They are the silent teachers of lessons not
contained in textbooks, and of wisdom that can only be
learned in their being present to us.

No matter how long a person lives, aging does not
sever ties with friends and family. As people grow older,
they have more time than ever before to develop relationships. Most older people long to see and be with family
and loved ones. But many people fail to visit their elderly
relatives and friends because of physical and mental
changes that often accompany old age. Forgetfulness, rep-
etitions of familiar stories and preoccupation with bodily
functions are not only boring and difficult to listen to, but
they are also painful reminders to family and friends that
their loved one is failing. In some cases, more acute illnesses add to the strain.

Old age brings out latent neurotic conditions or aggravates existing ones, so that it is not unusual to find some of the commoner symptoms of neurosis, such as anxiety, aggressive selfishness [and] intermittent depression.[5]

To live in the image and likeness of God is to provide them with companionship, love and care just as God promised to do for the Hebrew people throughout their lives and into old age:

> Listen to me, O house of Jacob,
>   all the remnant of the house of Israel,
> who have been borne by me from your birth,
>   carried from the womb;
> even to your old age I am God,
>   even when you turn gray I will carry you.
> I have made, and I will bear;
>   I will carry and will save (Is 46:3–4).

Most older people have led very active lives in society, in the workplace and in the church. Many of them suddenly find that no one seems to need them. When they want to talk, there is no one to listen; when they yearn to hear the voice of another person, there is no one there.

Psalm 71 appears to be a prayer of an aged worshiper who cries out to God in the midst of such suffering. This anguished person's self-concept is that of a "portent"—something that was feared, shunned and avoided like a plague:[6]

> I have been like a portent to many,
> but you are my strong refuge...
> Do not cast me off in the time of old age;
> do not forsake me when my strength is spent
>   (Ps 71:7, 9).

In addition to illness and isolation, many people in their declining years also experience financial strain in spite of our advanced society. Some elderly persons do without heat, eat less and try to sleep more in order to stretch their scanty income. Even though in their younger days they worked to give others dignity, they now work to survive in a world where they find themselves stripped of respect and concern. Even if there is little or nothing we can do financially for such a person, just showing compassion and concern helps to ease the stress. They may be able to relate to the economic vulnerability of Jesus in the gospels who lamented that he had no place to lay his head (Lk 9:58).

The early church grappled with the neglect of older persons and exhorted the church members to take care of their elderly family members:

> If a widow has children or grandchildren, let them first learn their religious duty to their own family and make some return to their parents; for this is acceptable in the eyes of God....If you do not provide for your relatives, and especially for your own family, you have disowned the faith and are worse than an unbeliever (1 Tim 5:4–8; RSV).

In the Graeco-Roman world, there was no social security system. Without family care, many older persons would have been abandoned in their time of need.

Faith Life and Aging

Because of the hurried pace of life in our Western culture, many people never set aside time for reflection. Their relationship with God may be nourished with their Sunday worship and with informal prayer while they go about their many duties. But time for reflection alone with God is considered a luxury, or even an impossibility, for the majority of people in their active years.

For all women and men, and especially for those persons whose lives have not been interwoven with periods of reflection, there is need in the years of old age to assess their lives. They need time to face the past with its virtues and sinfulness, not to grovel in guilt over failures, but to become ever more aware of and grateful for God's love, forgiveness and care. Such awareness often brings comfort as well as long overdue healing and relief for older people in their seemingly endless hours of solitude. St. Paul offers words that are especially wise and consoling to people in their later years:

> Do not worry about anything, but in everything by prayer and supplication with thanksgiving let your requests be made known to God. And the peace of God which surpasses all understanding will guard your hearts and your minds in Christ Jesus (Phil 4:6-7).

Because old age appears to bring with it the blessing of freedom of expression for many people, the visits of a pastoral minister become opportunities for which they frequently hunger. Older people need time to examine broken or weakened relationships that have not been healed, whether with family members, former friends, or God. Discussion of such issues with a pastor or spiritual adviser can bring peace and healing in many areas. Even the most thoughtful family members are often so preoccupied with the person's physical and emotional needs that they forget the spiritual aspect of caretaking.

In times of extreme loneliness, God is all that aging persons have to hold on to. Many elderly people would find great consolation in the words of the prophet Isaiah:

[Even] in your old age, I am God,
    even when you turn gray I will carry you.
I have made you, and I will bear you.
    I will carry you and save you (Is 46:4).

Old age, therefore, can be a fruitful time for people to deepen the spiritual dimension of their lives, a season in which they assess their relationship with God, other people and nature. Yet countless older persons have no one with whom to share their journey in faith.

The elderly need sensitive people who can accompany them on the inner journey, people who are willing to speak with them about God. For some aging persons whose lives have been less than exemplary, it is a frightening experience to look at the past. They need to hear and to understand that it is never too late to turn to God. One of the criminals crucified with Jesus received the promise of eternal life: "Today you will be with me in Paradise" (Lk 23:43). They may want help in being reconciled with God and other people, especially family members. Older people who were devout and religious most of their lives sometimes find themselves asking, "Where is God now?" They need someone to understand their feelings of abandonment and to help them make sense of their isolation and sufferings, both physical and spiritual.[7]

Aged persons often want and need people to listen to them and to assist them in sorting out what is worth living for, or what painful memories or broken relationships need healing. Msgr. Fahey, the director of Fordham University's Third Age Center, maintains that elderly persons also need a place where they can talk about the "pluses and minuses of older life...in the context of faith," a place where they can "reflect, pray and mutually support one another."[8] Msgr. Fahey contends:

We tend to take older persons for granted, when we really should be finding a broad approach to their spiritual concerns. They should be growing in their own interior life, their relationships with others, and their relationship with God. Unfortunately, our culture does not have the expectation of this kind of interior growth in later life, which can often be the seed for spirituality.[9]

Zechariah and Elizabeth, older persons in Luke's gospel, were examples of holiness (Lk 1:5–80). The aged widow, Anna, "never left the temple but worshiped there with fasting and prayer night and day" (Lk 2:38). Anna's old age was a ministry of prayer. Biblical personages such as these are good models to which people in their maturity can be called to imitate.

Many older people who are too ill to read or whose eyesight is failing like to have the Bible read to them. One woman observed that reading the Bible to her father had a calming effect on him. Since she lived at a distance and was unable to visit often, she taped parts of scripture and mailed them to him. In addition to the spiritual assistance, his daughter's voice enhanced the father's realization that his family cared about him even though they were unable to visit often. The woman selected psalms of thanksgiving, praise and hope. At special seasons, such as Christmas and Easter, she chose appropriate readings from the gospels. Since the gospel of Mark is the shortest of the gospels, she taped it in its entirety. Because of their life experiences, the elderly can easily relate to the characters in the gospels—the sick, the lame, the rich, the poor, fisherman, shepherds and soldiers.[10]

With a little encouragement, people in their later years would gladly fill the many hours they have alone with reflection on scripture. The Bible can take on new life and meaning at the stage of advanced maturity. Since death is very real to them, there is much with which they can identify, for example, Jesus in the Gethsemani scene in Mark's gospel. Jesus' experience of fear and distress as his own death became imminent can be especially consoling. Jesus wanted his close friends, the disciples, to stay awake and watch with him. Like Jesus, most people who live with impending death can relate to this need for companionship. They may easily identify with Jesus' struggle to be open to God's will:

> Abba Father, all things are possible to you. Take this cup away from me. Yet not what I will, but what you will (Mk 14:36).

The consoling words of Jesus at the last supper in John's gospel offer hope for the time when their suffering has ended. They may also help alleviate the fear of dying:

> Let not your hearts be troubled....I am going to prepare a place for you. And when I go and prepare a place for you, I will come again and take you to myself, that where I am you may be also (Jn 14:1-3; RSV).

Scripture gives us assurance that when the life of our earthly bodies ebbs away, there is new life for us:

> For we know that if the earthly tent we live in is destroyed, we have a building from God, a house not made with hands, eternal in the heavens. For in this tent we groan, longing to be clothed with our heavenly dwelling—if indeed, when we have taken it off we will not be found naked. For while we are still in this tent, we groan under our burden, because we wish not to be unclothed but to be further clothed, so that what is mortal may be swallowed up by life. He who has prepared us for this very thing is God, who has given us the Spirit as a guarantee (2 Cor 5:1-5; RSV).

Being present to people as they draw near the end of their lives affords one special moments of grace. I had the privilege of caring for my mother the year before she died.

She knew that she faced death at any moment, and I soon learned to speak about it with her. At first, I felt a bit uncomfortable and saddened when talking about her dying, but she appeared to be comfortable with the conversation. She admitted that while she looked foward to being with God and my Dad as well as with her extended family, she did have some fear of dying since, as she said, "I have never died before." She sometimes mused about what it would be like and how she hated to leave us, her children.

Two hours before my mother died, I sat with her on the side of the bed with my arms around her, and I treasure the memory of her peaceful expression. We both knew that death was imminent, and I was able to talk about it with her in spite of my tears. I recalled for her Jesus' words, "I will come and take you to myself" (Jn 14:3). Together, we prayed some familiar prayers of which she was particularly fond. As I kissed and caressed her, I felt as if my heart would break. I told her how I would miss her when God would come to take her home, but that I was willing to let her go to her family in heaven. I reminded her that her aching body would soon give way to her new spiritual body of which St. Paul speaks in one of his letters:

> What is sown is perishable, what is raised is imperishable. It is sown in dishonor, it is raised in glory. It is sown in weakness, it is raised in power. It is sown a physical body, it is raised a spiritual body (1 Cor 15:42–44; RSV).

My mother was deep in thought for a time and then said, "I surely do look forward to that. I wish I had that green suit to wear home," and then she chuckled. She was already happily anticipating that great celebration for which she wanted to be well-dressed. During the last year of her life, my mother taught me some of the most valuable lessons I will ever learn about living and dying.

Many older people have a deep faith life which they

have developed over the years, one that they could share if given the encouragement and opportunity. I heard a young college boy testify at the funeral of his grandmother that she had taught him more about prayer than anyone else. Ron, one of my former non-traditional students, often quoted his grandmother, and one of his favorites had to do with forgiveness: "My grandmother used to tell me, 'Never go to bed angry with anyone. Something might happen that you would never have a chance to make up.'" The wisdom of that woman lives on, and her grandson is passing it on not only to his children but to others as well.

> Older adults can be our mentors as they build on the blessings of their lifetime, confront and substitute for their losses and examine what is real and meaningful after their years of experience. But how often do we see a notice in a Church bulletin naming an older person available for counseling or shared prayer? How often do religious leaders tell young and middle aged members that there are older adults who could walk with them on their journey?[11]

The story of Joshua calling together the leaders of Israel in his old age and reminding them of God's faithfulness to them as a people is a good example of the wisdom of many of our senior persons:

> Joshua summoned all Israel, their elders and heads, their judges and officers, and said to them, "I am now old and well advanced in years; and you have seen all that your God has done...for your sake....Hold fast to your God.... And now I am about to go the way of all the earth, and you know in your hearts and souls, all of you, that not one thing has failed of all the good things that your God promised concerning you (Josh 23:2–16).

A Time for Making Choices

Older people realize that the years left them are certainly fewer than those through which they have lived. They often have choices to make, and they want support in making those choices. The autumn of life is a sacred time for persons who are mentally alert. They can direct their own lives during their last years, face the fact that death may soon open the door to eternal life, and make wise choices regarding the assets that they may still possess. For persons close to them, it is an opportunity to see things in their own lives in perspective, to realize that for them also life as we now experience it will someday come to an end. To miss the opportunity to accompany an elderly relative, friend or acquaintance in the process of getting things in order is to forfeit for oneself a graced moment and to deprive the loved one of support which they both need and most always desire.

Living arrangements is a matter in which elderly persons like to have a voice. Asking oneself the question, "How would I like to be treated were I in their shoes?" can help set an appropriate tone for approaching the subject. I believe that most people can accept what is best for them if they are accompanied through the process of decision-making by a person or persons who demonstrate love, sensitivity and respect for the individual. For many older people, living with family members may be feasible and desirable for both parties, while in other cases such things as the coming and going of younger people in the household may not be comfortable for either.

Whether the decision be for a nursing home or with family members when the elderly person can no longer function in an independent situation, he or she needs to have the opportunity to help make the decision. In cases where there is an option, it helps to ease anxiety to let the person know that if things don't work out, change is possible. If the option be for a nursing home, family and friends can make the adjustment to life there much easier with their frequent visits, letters and phone calls. Count-less people in such institutions feel that they have simply been dumped there and forgotten.

All people need time to work through their losses. As people grow older, they generally suffer many losses—death of one's spouse, friends, and siblings, loss of health, independence, or the ability to drive a car. As they deal with grief over these saddnesses that occur, they need to know that others mourn their losses with them, and that Jesus cried over the death of his friend (Jn 11:35). Empathy and compassion on the part of family and friends help to minimize the pain and loneliness involved.

One issue that every adult person needs to clarify, especially so the elderly, is the question of life-support systems. We can approach the subject by reassuring them of our love and our hope that we will have them with us for a long time. We need to know, however, in case they should become unable to speak for themselves, what their desires are about extraordinary means for keeping a person alive. Most people need some information about what constitutes extraordinary means or life-support sys-tems; thus a person may need to do some homework before discussing the issue with the loved one. Many peo-ple find that having a form designating a health care sur-rogate eases the anxiety of not being able at some point to make decisions about life-support systems.

Many aging persons want to discuss their funeral arrangements, a subject which is most often painful to loved ones and hence one which people often try to avoid. Yet for a person who has faced his or her mortality, the question is not a morbid one, but rather one that deals with the reality of life. One need not hide personal grief when the subject is broached, but we do need to muster the courage to discuss the matter with them. In all such matters, respect for the individual is paramount:

> You shall rise before the aged and show defer-ence to the old (Lev 19:32; RSV).

Shaping Our Declining Years

There is much we can do to shape the quality of old age for ourselves before it becomes a reality. Some psychologists maintain that facing the fact that we will probably reach old age, and cultivating a good self-concept, a positive attitude, a sense of humor and emotional stability are qualities which greatly enhance later-life adjustments.[12] There is a lot of truth in the saying, "As we now are, so shall we be when we are old." The book of Proverbs expresses this maxim thus:

> Train a lad in the way he ought to go, He will not swerve from it even in old age (Prov 22:6; RSV).

How one feels about oneself in relation to God and the world determines how a person accepts the process of aging. Good self-esteem based on the realization that one is loved by God and others is extremely important in order that a person *grow* older rather than be forced into old age by nature. However, if one's self-concept is based on such superficial things as sexuality, physical appearance, material possessions or achievement, old age will creep up like a thief to be despised, struggled against and denied.[13]

Nourishing a positive attitude in earlier years not only enhances one's later years but eases tension and anxiety throughout life. Learning trusting obedience to God in our daily life experiences by doing all that we can and then leaving the outcome to God is basic to a sound spirituality of aging. Such an attitude is expressed in the words of Jesus to Peter in the gospel of John:

> When you were young, you girded yourself and walked where you would; but when you are old, you will stretch out your hands, and another will gird you and carry you where you do not wish to go (Jn 21:18).

People who predict the worst scenario for every future possibility worry about things that most often never occur. Anxiety about what "might be" can be detrimental to both emotional and physical health. Chronic worriers generally determine a pattern for their later years of life, forgetting how faithful God is to us:

> Consider the lilies, how they grow: they neither toil nor spin; yet I tell you, even Solomon in all his glory was not clothed like one of these. But if God so clothes the grass of the field..., how much more will God clothe you—you of little faith (Lk 12:27–28).

A sense of humor can lessen the impact of life's adversities. Taking time to enjoy the light side of life, to laugh at the wit of other people and simply to laugh at one's own foibles cultivates a healthy disposition. If we learn to laugh when we are younger, old-age limitations will be less burdensome.

Many elderly persons who suffer from a lack of emotional stability developed unhealthy emotional responses throughout their lives. Learning to cope with the failings of other people, striving to accept oneself and other people without undue expectations, dealing with anger instead of "sweeping it under the rug," seeking counseling if circumstances warrant such—these life-patterns, or the lack of them, generally carry over into later life.

Developing one's faith life needs to be a lifelong process. If we look upon life as a time during which we come into harmony with God, other people and all of creation, even the signs of aging need not frighten us. They can be visible reminders to examine wherein harmony has already occurred in our lives and in which aspects there is still need for growth.

Summary

In our Western culture, old age is not generally valued. Therefore, instead of looking upon growing older as a natural life process which leads to eternal life, as we are taught in the New Testament, aging is more often than not perceived as a misfortune. Families and friends frequently avoid dealing with their loved ones' aging process and even neglect them rather than face what is happening in them.

A biblical spirituality cannot ignore this phase of life, neither one's own aging nor that of other people in society. People in their maturity offer us the opportunity to come to grips with our own mortality and to get our priorities in order. They remind us of the brevity of life, that life is a sojourn on this earth, and that our true home is with God.

While a person never knows at what moment death may occur, those who have reached maturity know that it cannot be long delayed. They need to be offered all the means that the Christian community possesses in order to mature spiritually and to face death as the entrance into life with God.

Even at its best, aging almost always involves painful experiences. However, a spirituality steeped in scripture can make growing older a time of growth and a longing for God.

As we turn to the next chapter on physical fitness, we find another aspect of spirituality that helps us to grow in God's image and likeness and thus prepares us for our later years.

For Further Reflection:

Ps 31
Lk 1:5–56; 2:36–88
Letter to the Philippians

SUGGESTED READINGS

Bumagin, Victoria. *Aging Is a Family Affair*. Thomas Y. Crowell, 1979.

Clements, William M. *Religion, Aging and Health*. Hawarth Press, 1989.

Dangott, Lillian R. *A Time to Enjoy: The Pleasures of Aging*. Prentice-Hall, 1979.

Dulin, Rachel Z. *A Crown of Glory: A Biblical View of Aging*. Paulist, 1988.

Finley, C.C.P., James F., *The Treasured Age*. Alba House, 1989.

Fisher, Edward. *Life in the Afternoon: Good Ways of Growing Older*. Paulist, 1987.

Fischer, Kathleen. *Winter Grace*. Paulist, 1985.

Gillman, John. "Going Home to the Lord," *The Bible Today* (Sept., 1982), 275–281.

Harris, J. Gordon. *Biblical Perspectives on Aging*. Fortress, 1987.

Huyck, Margaret Hellie. *Growing Older*. Prentice-Hall, 1974.

Kelly, Bill. "Sharing Scripture with Seniors," *Liguorian* 77 (April, 1989).

Koenig-Bricker, Woodeene. "Five Keys to Caregiving," *Liguorian* 79 (August, 1991) 20–23.

Mulgrove, Brother Ray. "A Spirituality of Aging," *Sisters Today* 63:4 (July, 1991) 286–288.

Sands, Florine C. "Senior Citizens Study the Bible," *The Bible Today* 30:4 (July, 1992) 218–223.

Unsworthy, Timothy. "What the Church Has Taught About Care for the Aged," *Salt* 9 (June, 1989) 14–17.

7

Keeping Fit for Life in Christ

*Do you not know that your body
is a temple of the Holy Spirit? (1 Cor 6:19).*

Our bodies are our constant companions every moment of our lives. They help us to express who we are to the world around us. With our bodies, we relate to other people and to God. Our bodies remind us when we need to rest, and they tell us when we can continue our activities. Our bodies are the channels through which we give and receive; they are our means of communication and transportation. They are important in the expression of our spirituality and our social relationships.

In the world of business, however, the body is treated almost exclusively in relation to its external appeal. The communication media serve the commercial world by advertising products to enhance physical appearance. Physical fitness centers compete in quality equipment in order to offer the most enticing opportunities to keep the body trim and healthy. Creams and lotions ensnare millions who consciously or unconsciously search for the fountain of youth. Vitamins offer the hope of prolonging life. Foods of one kind and then another become fads in their turn as they rise to first place with their claims to deter fatal diseases. Few people can resist all such guarantees to enhance the quality and span of life.

Sarx and Soma

Can there be a Christian dimension to all this concern for the well-being of the body? Making the body attractive is not necessarily negative. Our body is our first introduction to other people. If people are initially

attracted to us rather than repulsed, they may more
quickly listen to us and take seriously our Christian way
of life. Moreover, sensible care for one's body is firmly
based in Christian tradition.

In Pauline theology, the body is a central theme.
Sometimes "body" refers to our flesh and blood bodies,
sometimes to the church, and at other times to our whole
beings. Paul tells us that we are delivered from the body
of sin and death (Rom 6:6). Our salvation came through
the body of Christ on the cross (Eph 2:14-16). We are
incorporated into the church, the body of Christ (1 Cor
12:27). The church is sustained through the eucharist
which is his body (1 Cor 11:23-26). Through our bodies,
we manifest Christ to the world (2 Cor 4:10) and glorify
him (1 Cor 6:20). Our bodies will be raised to a likeness
of his glorious body (1 Cor 15:44).[1]

In Paul's letters, originally written in Greek, we find
two words for "body"—*soma* and *sarx*. Although at times
Paul uses the words interchangeably, more often *soma*
expresses the human person or the whole self, while *sarx*
refers to the material, earthbound, flesh and blood body.[2]

Paul's notion of the wholeness of the person, (which
he derived from his Jewish background rather than his
Greek culture), is verified in the common human experience of wellness and sickness. The state of either affects
the whole person, not just the material body. For example,
when one is well, there is a sense of wholeness of being.
Communication with God and other people appears to
come with ease. Physical and mental activities are undertaken with feelings of pleasure and achievement. On the
other hand, when a person is ill, he or she experiences
something in addition to physical sickness. There is a
sense of self-sickness that affects the entire person. Once a
source of consolation and satisfaction, the ability to pray,
to interact with other people, or to concentrate becomes
difficult and sometimes impossible. Even though we
often speak of spirit and body in our Christian tradition,

our human existence defies compartmentalization or isolation of either.

Recognize Your Dignity

Paul's letters provide an early Christian ethic for care of the body based on the dignity acquired at baptism. In the letter to the Corinthians, Paul highlights the body's holiness:

> The body is meant not for fornication but for the Lord, and the Lord for the body. And God raised the Lord and will also raise us by his power. Do you not know that your bodies are members of Christ? Should I therefore take the members of Christ and make them members of a prostitute? Never!...Or do you not know that your body is a temple of the Holy Spirit within you, which you have from God, and that you are not your own? For you were bought with a price; therefore glorify God in your body (1 Cor 6:13–15, 19–20).

Immorality reaches the very core and affects the whole person; it is unworthy of Jesus Christ who purchased us with his own blood (1 Cor 7:23). Once bought by Christ (1 Cor 6:20), we belong to him. Christ entered the domain of sin and death in a body of flesh. He redeemed and transfigured it: "The Lord for the body" (1 Cor 6:13), as Paul expressed it. He has honored us by making us dwellings of his Spirit and thus continues to live in the church through us. Hence, God is rightly to be glorified in the body (1 Cor 6:13) whether by life or by death (Phil 1:20).

Paul's use of the temple as an analogy for the body is linked with the notion of the glorious temple in Jerusalem. The temple was looked upon as God's dwelling place in the midst of the people (1 Kgs 8:13). No longer the stone and mortar of the temple, but the very

living body of the Christian is to be a visible manifestation of God's dwelling among human beings. Unlike the
Jerusalem temple to which some people had to travel
long distances, and hence visit infrequently, the
Christian can take the loving presence of the risen Christ
to the ends of the earth and to every person encountered
in daily life. Sin, therefore, has no rightful home in our
bodies (Rom 6:12).

Paul speaks of the privilege of Christ-bearing in
poetic terms:

> We have this treasure in earthenware vessels to
> show that the measureless power belongs to
> God and not to us" (2 Cor 4:2; RSV).

Were it otherwise, we could easily forget the source of
our strength and attribute it to our own self-sufficiency.
So powerful is God's work in and through our weakness
that Paul could say, "When I am weak, then I am strong"
(2 Cor 12:10). Paul goes on to list the adversities that his
own "earthen vessel" has endured by the power of
Christ. He adds that we are "always carrying in the body
the death of Jesus so that the life of Jesus may be mani-
fested in our bodies" (2 Cor 4:8–10). Because of this conviction, Paul could write from imprisonment:

> I want you to know, beloved, that what has hap-
> pened to me has really served to advance the
> gospel, so that it has become known throughout
> the whole praetorian guard and to all the rest
> that my imprisonment is for Christ (Phil 1:12–
> 13).

The Christian is never in isolation from the entire
"body of Christ," the church:

> For just as the body is one and has many mem-
> bers, and all the members of the body, though

many, are one body, so it is with Christ. For in the one Spirit we were all baptized into one body—Jews or Greeks, slaves or free—and we were all made to drink of one Spirit.... Now you are the body of Christ and individually members of it (1 Cor 12:12-13, 27).

In his use of the body as a metaphor for the church, Paul probably drew upon an ancient philosophical idea about the moral unity that exists within a group that works toward a common goal.[3] But the body expressed far more for Paul than merely a union of people working together for the welfare of the whole group. For Paul, the body is made up of intricate systems, different though they are, which work together as a unity for the good of the whole. So it is with the church, a body made up of many members of differing backgrounds, races and colors united by the Spirit of Christ alive in us. If one member suffers, we all suffer together (1 Cor 12:26).

According to Pauline thought, the body has a cultic dimension, that is, we use it in worship. In his letter to the Roman church, Paul urges Christians to "present their bodies as living sacrifices, holy and acceptable to God" (Rom 12:1). So profound is this offering that the apostle calls it their "spiritual worship." Paul is saying that as followers of Christ their lives are to replace the animal sacrifices that were first slain and then burnt in Jewish worship of God in the temple. No longer were the dead bodies of animals to be used as sacrifice; instead, the living bodies of committed Christians going about their daily lives were to serve as sacred offerings in the midst of an imperfect and hostile world (Rom 8:7). Their selfless lives were to be consumed, not by fire as were the animal sacrifices, but little by little in the exercise of their talents and gifts for the good of the community (Rom 12:1-8). By their generous love for one another (Rom 12:9-13) as well as for those who waged persecution against them (Rom 12:14-21), they were to be metaphorically consumed.[4] In this way, their bodies would give glory to God as living sacrifices. They would thereby provide worship which did not cease with a religious ritual that was bound to a specific geographical location.

Discipline the Body

> If any want to become my followers, let them deny themselves and take up their cross and follow me. For those who want to save their life will lose it, and those who lose their life for my sake and the sake of the gospel will save it (Mk 8:34–35).

Followers of Christ cannot be preoccupied with self and personal interests. Instead, their concerns are to be centered on those of Jesus in the gospel. Just as Jesus' concern for presenting the goodness of God even to sinners and outcasts brought him suffering, and ultimately death, so also will it be for his disciples. Laying down one's life is the highest degree of self-denial.

A spirit of self-denial or asceticism cannot be achieved overnight. The body cries out for indulgence. Nevertheless, it is discipline that prepares us to serve Christ in other people. Discipline frees the body and the spirit so that we may experience more authentic life, a life in union with Christ Jesus. A life of asceticism emerges from an attitude in which a person affirms that material things are God's gift to humanity.[5] Far from demeaning the body, asceticism is an anti-consumerism attitude in which a person freely rejects the autonomous use of material things as a means directed to intimate awareness and union with God, and not because they are considered bad.[6]

One type of asceticism found in scripture is fasting from food for a time. Moses fasted forty days and forty nights before receiving the commandments from God on

Mt. Horeb (Dt 9:9). After being fed by an angel of God, Elijah refrained from eating for forty days (1 Kgs 19:1-8). Jesus fasted forty days and forty nights before beginning his public ministry (Mt 4:2; Lk 4:2).

The purpose of all types of asceticism is the emptying of our minds and hearts of all distractions that inhibit our communication with God. In Jesus' day, pious Jews fasted twice a week. In Mark's gospel, some of the people were scandalized that Jesus' disciples fasted infrequently:

> Why do John's disciples and the disciples of the Pharisees fast, but your disciples do not fast (Mk 2:18)?

Jesus responded by comparing his coming to a wedding banquet and asking:

> Can the wedding guests fast while the bridegroom is with them? The days will come when the bridegroom is taken away from them, and then they will fast in that day (Mk 2:19–20).

Fasting had obviously not profited the Pharisees; it did not open their eyes to understand that Jesus was the messiah. The value of fasting may still be measured by the extent that it helps us to recognize Jesus in the people and events of our daily lives.

The practice of authentic asceticism does not demean the body. St. Anthony of the Desert (third century), hermit and ascetic though he was, showed a clear respect for the body. He advised the Greek philosophers that it was only fitting to admire created things, but not to deify them. When people visited or joined the hermit, Anthony provided a varied diet for them. He viewed the body as a medium of revelation of the incarnate Christ.[7] Where the body/person was present, there Christ was made present to the people.

Thomas Merton, a modern day contemplative, valued the practices of asceticism as a means of liberation from routine existence. The purpose of self-discipline, he maintained, is to deepen and expand our capacities for experience of the world and people about us, to heighten our awareness of all of creation, and to come to a better understanding and love of God, ourselves and other people.[8] In the history of Christianity, asceticism in that sense has played a major role in fashioning holy people from John the Baptist (Mk 1:6–8) down to the present.

Today, however, many people consider asceticism a relic of the past and appropriate only for those in cloisters and recluses. Yet quality of life requires that asceticism be revived. Our environment has become noisy, crowded and polluted. Discipline of body and spirit has given way to self-indulgence, to channeling our body's energy to overwork, achievement of power, sexual promiscuity, drug addiction and overeating. These masochistic practices work havoc in the body, dull the life of the Spirit, and inhibit our awareness of the Source of all life. Indeed, these very addictions seek to replace the Source of life. Their object is immediate pleasure. This "agenda of the flesh is hard on the body and the soul, inflicting the anxiety that at any moment its object of desire will fail to provide the large and real emotion constantly required for feeling fully alive."[9]

Asceticism can also lead to a deeper appreciation of self and God's presence within us. Thomas Merton quotes an ascetic rabbi of the seventeenth century:

No matter how low you may have fallen in your own esteem, bear in mind that if you delve deeply into yourself you will discover holiness there. A holy spark resides there which, through repentance, you may fan into a consuming flame, which will burn away the dross of unholiness and unworthiness.[10]

Because asceticism minimizes our focus on material things, it silences the body, so to speak, and predisposes us to be aware of Christ's presence in us. Confronted with his loving presence, we become like Simon Peter—acutely aware of our unworthiness. "Depart from me," Peter pleaded, "for I am a sinful person" (Lk 5:8). As we face our sinfulness, the affirming words of Jesus in John's gospel echo in our hearts: "You are my friends.... You did not choose me, but I chose you" (Jn 15:14–16). So loved are we by our God that Jesus "bought us with a price" (1 Cor 6:20), the price of his own life.

The practice of asceticism (i.e., fasting, denying oneself legitimate pleasures) helps free the body to share in the life of the Spirit. Since we live in a society in which we are fed on a constant diet of distraction and entertainment, there is a need to focus our energy on the Source of our being. If our desires and ambitions become the focus of our lives, they tend to "blind us, weaken us, unnerve us, make us cowards, conformists, hypocrites."[11] As St. Paul asserts, "The body was not made for immorality, but for the Lord, and the Lord for the body" (1 Cor 6:13). Ascetic practices help us in the orientation of our lives. Because our bodies are integrally connected with our souls, our souls benefit or suffer depending on the agenda set by the flesh (the *sarx*). Whatever ascetic practices we choose must enhance the life of both the body and the soul. Ascetic practices that are aimed at punishing the body negate the sacredness of the body: "Do you not know that your body is a temple of the Holy Spirit within you which you have from God" (1 Cor 6:19)?

Temporary ascetic practices make us aware of our debilitating addictions. Fasting even for one meal can bring to consciousness one's addiction to food. Short periods of fasting, such as three days, are actually good for the body since it allows the body to rest from constant metabolic exercise. Fasting from television and radio for a time can alert us to the havoc of having our attention continually manipulated by external forces.

Ascetical practices help us to focus our energy on God as the source of our being.[12]

This kind of temporary asceticism has been practiced by hermits and monks throughout history. Often their asceticism was directed at some particular fault or temptation. The ascetics warned their disciples not to neglect their bodies. Athanasius tells us that St. Anthony emerged from the desert with his body looking much the same as when he went in twenty years before.[13]

Fasting from worry is another type of asceticism that benefits the whole being. Living the present moment and abandoning ourselves to God's loving providence helps to eliminate worry about things that may never happen in the future. Most things people fret about, even to the point of getting sick, never occur. Regarding our cares and anxieties, Jesus had this to say:

> I tell you, do not be anxious about your life, what you shall eat, nor about your body what you shall put on. For life is more than food, and the body more than clothing. Consider the ravens: they neither sow nor reap, they have neither storehouse nor barn, and yet God feeds them. Of how much more value are you than the birds! And which of you by being anxious can add a cubit to your life span? If then you are not able to do as small a thing as that, why are you anxious about the rest? Consider the lilies, how they grow; they neither toil nor spin; yet I tell you, even Solomon in all his glory was not arrayed like one of these. But if God so clothes the grass which is alive in the field today and tomorrow is thrown into the oven, how much more will he clothe you! (Lk 12:22–28)

Asceticism is a method, not a goal in itself. A disciplined way of life, however, does have immediate goals such as overcoming addictions, focusing our energy, or intensifying our awareness. The ultimate goal of asceticism is to prepare us to enter more fully aware into union with God, a union that Jesus made possible.

Risk the Body

Legitimate care of the body does not rule out risk for the Christian, however. Like Jesus, a person must sometimes endure the crucible of suffering as a result of Christian involvement in the world.

St. Paul underwent much suffering and illness for the sake of taking Christ and his message to peoples of many lands and cultures. In one of his letters to the Corinthian church, Paul speaks frankly of the physical trials he had borne during his mission of spreading the gospel. In a beating from his own Jewish people, he received "forty lashes less one," that is, one whiplash short of the maximum number allowed by the Jewish law in Deuteronomy 5:3 for a person judged guilty. Three times Paul was beaten with rods (a form of Roman punishment), and once he was stoned. He suffered the perils of shipwreck three times, and he knew well the terrible fear of being adrift at sea for a night and a day. In his extensive travels (a round trip from Jerusalem to Corinth involved some 3000 miles), he faced the dangers of crossing rivers, the threat of bandit-infested lands, and even persecution at the hands of his own Jewish people as well as from the Gentiles. The cities were no escape; there, too, he suffered as an outsider. He also encountered the dangers of the desert, which were considerable in the first century. Often unable to reach lodging, he spent nights outside, unprotected from the elements, sleepless, hungry and cold. Anxiety over the churches he had founded was added to the apostle's physical pain (2 Cor 11:24-28).

These sufferings were of such intensity that Paul speaks of them in Galatians 6:17 as "marks of Jesus" which he bore in his body. Generally, the word "marks" in Greek indicated brandings imposed on slaves. Paul thus considered his adversities (Gal 4:13) and his physical persecutions (2 Cor 11:25) as brandings which marked him as a slave for the sake of Christ. His body, therefore, was living witness to his love for Christ and his tireless dedication to spreading the gospel.

Paul's idea of re-presenting Christ in our bodies is exemplified in the awareness of German students in England after World War II. One of the cathedrals had suffered damage from the Luftwaffe bombings, and German students helped in its rebuilding. A statue of Jesus bearing the inscription, "Come unto me," had lost its hands. The workers agreed that the statue could be patched up except for the hands. The students finally reached a decision—they would not attempt to restore the hands. Rather, they would change the inscription which remains to this day: "Christ has no hands but ours."[14]

Paul's experience taught him that a stance for Christ-centered values often puts the sincere Christian in conflict with people of opposite views. We may have to bear insults on account of our love for the risen Christ. In his letter to the Romans, Paul speaks of the tension thus created as a "warring situation." The genuine Christian who belongs to the realm of the Spirit is faced with hostility from those who reject the standards of Christ (Rom 8:1–11). Yet the sufferings one must endure for the sake of Christ are made bearable by the fact that we do not suffer alone; we suffer together with Christ. As co-heirs with him, we share not only his glory and relationship with God as parent, but also the path of his suffering:

> For all who are led by the Spirit of God are children of God. For you did not receive a spirit of slavery to fall back into fear, but you have received a spirit of adoption... It is that very Spirit bearing witness with our spirit that we are children of God, and if children, then heirs, heirs of God and joint heirs with Christ—if, in

fact, we suffer with him so that we may also be glorified with him (Rom 8:14-17).

Risks that Christians face in the United States today may be more financial than directly physical. A stand for a safe environment for future generations; a challenge to the electorate to reduce the production of weapons and their sales to other nations in order that world hunger might be alleviated; a cry that housing be made available for homeless people—all such concerns and consequent actions may in the long run diminish the Christian's comfort. But no matter how we may have to suffer, Paul assures the Christian community that no power whatsoever "will be able to separate us from the love of God in Christ Jesus our Lord" (Rom 8:38-39). "If God is for us, who is against us" (Rom 8:31)?

Plan Your Future

> He will transform the body of our humiliation
> that it may be conformed to the body of his
> glory (Phil 3:21).

The final goal of the body (*soma*) also validates its regard and care. For the believer, death itself is not the grand finale but only a passage from corruptibility. We share this condition with all of creation, until we reach incorruptibility:

> Creation itself will be set free from its bondage
> to decay and obtain the glorious liberty of the
> children of God (Rom 8:21).

Death only intensifies the privileged status of the faithful Christian as God's children. Paul uses birthing language in Romans 8, a language of hope and expectation, to speak of our waiting for this transformation. We are "groaning in travail" (8:22) for "the redemption of our

bodies" (8:23). Already God's children and hence brothers and sisters of Jesus Christ (8:11), we await the glory
yet to come that is ours as baptized Christians (8:11). That
realization enabled Paul to write from prison with a
sense of detachment: "For me to live is Christ; to die is
gain" (Phil 1:20b–21).

Paul compares our physical bodies with our resurrected bodies by use of the analogy of a seed and its relation to a plant. A tiny seed holds within it the secret
mystery of a future plant. The seed remains a simple
seed without exterior signs of an impressive future until
it is put into the soil and dies. Only then does it spring
forth into a plant which is much more striking than was
ever suggested by the unimpressive seed:

> What is sown is perishable, what is raised is
> imperishable. It is sown in dishonor, it is raised
> in glory. It is sown in weakness, it is raised in
> power. It is sown a physical body, it is raised a
> spiritual body (1 Cor 15:42–44).

Summary

Paul looks with reverence upon the human body, that
is, the *soma* or the whole person. Using the metaphor of
the temple, he regards it as the means by which we make
Christ present to the world. In carrying out this sacred
charge, however, the body is vulnerable to the hostility of
the world that refuses to accept the gospel of Jesus Christ.
Although the body suffers and will eventually die, it
awaits impending glory as a resurrected body.

For the Christian, it is both a duty as well as a virtue
to care for the body. Reasoning from Paul's perspective of
the body's dignity, it is only logical that proper diet, rest
and exercise are but necessary means of helping make us
more fit for the mission that is ours as believers in
Christ. To be "temples" or Christ-bearers, to live our lives
in service of others and thus offer continuous sacrificial

worship of God, to undergo the brandings or marks of slaves in service of Christ as a consequence of witnessing to the gospel—all require physical endurance.

Sensible attention to and care of the body not only enhance the effectiveness of our Christian mission, but proper exercise and rest also serve as deterrents to burn-out in ministry as well as in the struggle to live the Christian life according to the gospel. Regard for the condition of our bodies will be a constant reminder that whatever be our call as Christians, our work is mission in the name of Jesus Christ and not just a job to be accomplished. Machines can do tasks, but only persons can carry out the mission of taking Christ to the people they encounter each day of their lives.

In the following chapter, we will examine loyalty in relationships as another important area of the spiritual life.

For Further Reflection:

> 1 Cor 15:1–58
> Eph 3:14–21
> 1 Thes 4:1–12

Suggested Readings

Ashley, O.P., Benedict M., *Theologies of the Body: Humanist and Christian.* The Pope John Center Press, 1985.

Brand, Paul and Philip Young, *Fearfully and Wonderfully Made.* Zondervan, 1980.

Galipeau, Steven A. *Transforming Body and Soul.* Paulist, 1990.

Carroll, William E. "It's My Body: I Can Do What I Want With It," *The Canadian Catholic Review* 8 (Apr. 1990) 153–54.

Maloney, S.J., George. *Following Jesus in the Real World: Asceticism Today.* Clarity Publishing, Inc., 1966.

Merton, Thomas. *Contemplation in a World of Action.* Doubleday, 1973.

Miles, Margaret R. *Fullness of Life: Historical Foundations for a New Asceticism.* Westminster, 1981.

Robinson, John A. T. *The Body: A Study in Pauline Theology.* SCM Press, 1966.

Ryan, Thomas. *Wellness, Spirituality and Sports* (Paulist, 1986).

_____, *Disciplines for Christian Living* (Paulist, 1993).

8

Fidelity in Relationships

Give thanks to God who is good,
whose faithfulness endures forever (Ps 136:1).

The story of Noah and the flood in the Old Testament is a story of God's fidelity to humankind. Noah, even though he was a good man and walked with God, was a mere human being (Gen 6:9-10). Why did God need to give him and his descendants a sign of fidelity? Couldn't God simply have called it quits with the flood and let it go at that? Indeed, God could have handled it that way, but the narrative seems to indicate that they were friends. Noah walked with God. The story implies that it was important to God that Noah be able to trust God and not be afraid that at some unforeseen time, God would turn on him and just wipe him off the face of the earth. So God put a "bow" in the sky to remind Noah and all of his descendants that they could always trust God's faithfulness to them.

The Fidelity of God

The fidelity of God is at the heart of all fidelity. God is not a "tit for tat" God. Regardless of the extent of our infidelities, we can always count on God's faithful and steadfast love. No matter how much human relationships may have wounded and deceived us, there is always one whose love for us will never change.

The grass withers, the flowers fade; but the word of our God will stand forever (Is 40:8).

The psalms and prophets repeatedly proclaim the

139

permanence of God's fidelity. Ancient Israelite confessions of faith show that from of old God's people had experienced that quality of fidelity in their relationship with God.

> Yahweh is compassionate and gracious,
>   long-suffering and ever faithful (Ps 103:8; NJB).

> It is good to give thanks to
>   Yahweh,
>   to sing praises to your name,
>   O Most High;
>   to declare your steadfast love in
>   the morning,
>   and your faithfulness by night,
>   to the music of the flute and the
>   harp,
> to the melody of the lyre (Ps 92:1-3).

> Your steadfast love, O Yahweh,
>   extends to the heavens,
> your faithfulness to the clouds.
> . . . .
> How precious is your steadfast
>   love, O God!
>   All people may take refuge in
>   the shadow of your wings.
> They feast on the abundance of
>   your house,
>   and you give them drink from
>   the river of your delights (Ps 36:5-8).

The prophet Isaiah was so touched by the faithfulness of our God that he compared it to that of a mother who is constantly aware of the child that is feeding at her breast or one that is still growing in her womb:

> Can a woman forget her nursing child,
>   or show no compassion for the

child in her womb?
Even these may forget,
> yet I will not forget you.
See, I have inscribed you on the
> palms of my hands (Is 49:15-16).

The prophet Hosea expressed God's faithfulness in terms of an intimate bond or relationship like that of marriage. The Israelites had been vacillating in their relationship with God; they were faithful at times, but they turned to other gods when convenient. Hosea understood God's love for the people to be similar to his own love for his unfaithful wife, Gomer. God's faithful love did not cease even though Israel's actions were like that of a harlot. God's passionate love for this people resounds in the tender and nostalgic words of the prophet:

Like grapes in the wilderness,
> I found Israel.
Like the first fruit on the fig tree,
> in its first season,
> I saw your ancestors....
When Israel was a child, I loved him,
> And out of Egypt I called my son.
The more I called them,
> the more they went from me;
they kept sacrificing to the Baals,
> and offering incense to idols.
Yet it was I who taught Ephraim to walk,
> I took them up in my arms;
> but they did not know that I healed them.
I led them with cords of human kindness,
> with bands of love.
I was to them like those
> who lift infants to their cheeks.
I bent down to them
> and fed them (Hos 9:10; 11:1-4).

The people of Israel had failed in their fidelity to God, but God's love for them never wavered. The author of 2 Timothy speaks of God's faithful love expressed by Jesus Christ in similar terms: "If we are faithless, he remains faithful—for he cannot deny himself" (2 Tim 2:13).

The loyalty shown us by God in scripture provides a model for assessing our own fidelity in relationships. God's love for us is a totally disinterested love. God does not love us in order to be loved in return, but, as John states, God loves us in order "that we might live" (1 Jn 4:9). God's desire "that we might live" is the desire that we live eternally in happiness with God.

The covenant that God made with the Israelites in the Old Testament is characterized by consistent fidelity and mercy. Unlike human beings whose patience tends to wear thin and eventually evaporates when things don't improve, God never gives up on us. God remains faithful and ready to forgive us regardless of the seriousness and frequency of our infidelities (Ex 34:6; Num 14:19; Jer 3:12).

Jesus, God's Fidelity

Jesus, God-become-human among us, was the living embodiment of God's faithful love for us. Throughout his ministry, Jesus repeatedly stressed that God was faithful in loving and forgiving us. Such gratuitous love was difficult for the Pharisees and scribes to understand. They promoted the notion that observance of the law elicited God's love. Therefore, they frequently found themselves in conflict with Jesus. On one occasion, these religious leaders complained that Jesus ate with sinners. In the Palestinian culture of Jesus' day, eating at table with someone was tantamount to unconditional acceptance of the person. To the dismay of his critics, that was exactly the message that Jesus wished to convey.

In response to the consternation of the Pharisees and scribes, Jesus told them this parable:

Which one of you, having a hundred sheep and losing one of them, does not leave the ninety-nine in the wilderness and go after the one that is lost until he finds it? When he has found it, he lays it on his shoulders and rejoices. And when he comes home, he calls together his friends and neighbors, saying to them, "Rejoice with me, for I have found my sheep that was lost." Just so, I tell you, there will be more joy in heaven over one sinner who repents than over ninety-nine righteous persons who need no repentance (Lk 15:4–7).

Notice that there is not the least indication that the sheep cries out in distress or tries to find its way back. The initiative is totally on the part of the shepherd. As absurd as it may sound, the keeper of the sheep leaves the huge flock and goes off to search for one single stray sheep. When he finds it, he is so happy that he lifts the sheep up on his shoulders and carries this heavy weight home with him. Then the shepherd becomes even more extravagant according to human standards; he calls in the neighbors to celebrate his finding this one insignificant sheep. "Most unlikely," we might say. And indeed we are right. Most human beings would not go to such extremes if they had ninety-nine more sheep who caused no trouble and stayed with the flock. That is precisely the point Jesus wanted to make; only God could care that much for one lowly person who walks away. Observe the repetition of "rejoice" and the emphasis on "joy" in the parable. Jesus is telling us that God is ecstatic when a sinner is found and metaphorically rests on God's shoulder.

In his efforts to convey the reliability of God's unconditional love for us, Jesus also compared God to a woman who lost a coin of insignificant value. She swept the house and searched until she found the small coin. Like the shepherd, she also called in the neighbors to celebrate the retrieval of something that most people would consider extremely unimportant (Lk 15:8-10). According to Jesus, who came to show us what God is really like, no person lacks significance in the loving eyes of our God. Regardless of the insignificant value that the world may try to impose on us, God's faithful love perceives in each one of us a person of great worth.

Called To Be Faithful

Our spirituality is the sum of our relationships to God, self, other people and the earth. Symbols of faithfulness that permeate our universe provide inspiration and nourishment for fidelity in all our relationships. The stars consistently hold their course in the galaxy; the sun rises and sets even when hidden by clouds; day faithfully gives way to night; one season follows another in dependable order. These patterns occur without failure, and we never have to wonder whether or not they will happen. Wherever we turn, we can see and experience in creation the fidelity of our God and creator.

The patterns of fidelity that are obvious in nature, however, are not so prevalent in society. Everywhere people turn, they are confronted with challenges and failures in fidelity. Infidelity pervades marriages, friendships, the church, the workplace and the political arena. Marriages deteriorate more and more frequently. Deep and lasting friendships are no longer the experience of a majority of people. Long-term commitments are undertaken less often and abandoned more quickly. Faithfulness to one's work is sometimes looked upon by co-workers as ingratiation, or "brown-nosing," to use the popular term. Today employers and employees are faced with issues of loyalty which were nonexistent in the workplace of the past. Fidelity to the electorate has eluded all too many politicians at every level of government. Loyalty to one's country is most often measured in terms of response to military service and almost never in terms of prophetic loyalty which calls for justice. It may well be that human fidelity is facing its greatest challenge in history.

The media capitalize on issues that interest their audiences. If we can judge from the response, the public appears to be extremely interested in the infidelities of public figures and fictitious characters of movies and television. There seems to be an obsession with the unfaithful, while at the same time most people value some kind of fidelity in their own lives.

Fidelity to God

In the midst of the lack of faithfulness that we hear about, see, and sometimes experience, Christians have an opportunity and mission that has its roots in baptism. The Spirit by whom we live calls us and graces us with courage to witness to fidelity in the world:

> When the Counselor comes, whom I shall send you from the Father, even the Spirit of truth, who proceeds from the Father, he will bear witness to me; and you also are witnesses (Jn 15:26-27; RSV).

As Christians, we never stand alone in living the fidelity to which we are called in baptism. No matter where we may be—whether at home, among friends, or in the workplace—we have the opportunity, through the Spirit who lives in us, to let Christ's faithfulness reflect through us to those around us. The Spirit's presence and assistance will enable us to encourage, enhance, and promote fidelity in the lives of others.

> The Consoler, the Holy Spirit, whom the Father will send in my name, he will teach you all things, and bring to your remembrance all that I have said to you (Jn 14:16-20; RSV).

Our own faithfulness to God is measured by the degree that we strive to live in the image and likeness of God. To live in God's image and likeness is to love and treat others as we would like to be treated. Our love for God cannot be separated from our love for other people. The author of the first letter of John states:

> God is love, and those who abide in love abide in God, and God abides in them....We love because God first loved us. Those who say, "I love God," and hate their brothers and sisters, are liars; for those who do not love a brother or sister whom they have seen, cannot love God whom they have not seen (1 Jn 4:16–20; RSV).

Our fidelity to other people, then, is the measure of our love for God. Jesus is the teacher par excellence. We learn how he loved from the gospels. Even when his witness to God's love and forgiveness of us brought the threat of death from the religious leaders, he was faithful to his mission of love among us.

The compassionate Jesus serves as a model for faithful relationships with all people, especially with friends. His compassion is particularly striking when his closest disciples fail him. In the gospels of Matthew, Mark, and Luke, the disciples abandon Jesus in his greatest hour of need. Nevertheless, Jesus remains faithful to them. At the last supper, after his prediction that the disciples would all flee in light of his arrest and sufferings, Luke reports that Jesus spoke the most astoundingly kind words to these same disciples: "You are the ones who have continued with me in all my trials" (Lk 22:28; RSV). These were words of faithful friendship and consolation that they could remember once they realized their great infidelity to Jesus. There were no words of shame, no subtle intent to lay a guilt trip on the disciples. Jesus was putting into practice his own teaching—that we be compassionate to people who fail us just as God is compassionate to us (Lk 6:36).

Forgiveness is a necessary component of any relationship. Human beings will sometimes make mistakes just as Peter and the disciples in the gospel failed their friend, Jesus. In spite of their infidelity at the time of his greatest need, Jesus did not hold a grudge. He wanted these same disciples to know immediately when he had risen from the dead. In one of the post-resurrection appearances in the gospel of John, Jesus waits for the disciples on the shore and has breakfast prepared for them when they arrive. There is no chiding, no bitterness; Jesus' only concern is for them. Peter is given the opportunity to heal the pain of his threefold denial. Three times Jesus asks Peter, "Do you love me?" Three times (corresponding to the three times he had denied his relationship to Jesus), Peter affirms his love (John 21:15-17).

The School of Fidelity

As Christians, our relationship with Christ has the potential to vitalize all our relationships. St. Paul tells us that in baptism God's love was poured into our hearts through the Holy Spirit (Rom 5:5). God's love became a part of us; therefore, we are capable of loving with God's own faithful love. For that kind of love to become active in our lives, however, we need time alone with Jesus, time to ponder his way of being faithful as shown us in the gospels. In nourishing our friendship with Jesus, the One who set no limits on his love, we learn to love as he did. Only then will we appreciate how Jesus' own union with God permeated his relationships with human beings:

Abide in me as I abide in you. Just as the branch cannot bear fruit by itself unless it abides in the vine, neither can you unless you abide in me. I am the vine, you are the branches....As the Father has loved me, so I have loved you; abide in my love (Jn 15:4-9).

In relating to Jesus Christ, we encounter the perfect model of unconditional love, compassion, understanding and forgiveness. "The one who calls you is faithful," Paul tells us (1 Thess 5:24). He is faithful in his love for us from the first moment of our existence. He is faithful in his compassion for us when we suffer the hardships of life. He is faithful in his understanding and forgiveness when in our weakness we sin. These are the lessons of fidelity in relationships that Jesus teaches us in the gospel. St. Paul summarizes this fidelity in the following exhortation:

> [Be] kind to one another, tenderhearted, forgiving one another as God in Christ has forgiven you (Eph 4:32).

Biblical fidelity, however, is not a model for never ending a relationship. In fact, in order to be loyal to the other person involved as well as to oneself, it may be necessary to end a relationship, especially if it be mutually destructive. In the book of Ruth, Naomi's daughter-in-law, Ruth, would not abandon her mother-in-law. She even left her own homeland and went to a foreign country with Naomi. Orpah, on the other hand, accepted the freedom that her mother-in-law extended to them to stay in their own land and marry a person from among their own people. Nevertheless, a faithful person will never take any relationship lightly.[1] If a person places great value on faithfulness to people, she or he sets the tone for relating faithfully to God and to all of creation.

Fr. Bernard Häring, a moral theologian, suggests that non-violence is the key to sound interpersonal relationships. A non-violent person meets both friends and foes alike with the non-violence of Christ. She or he approaches others with a mind open to dialogue and with an attitude that invites a common search for more light and the best solution to conflicts. A non-violent person considers all of creation the object of peace and love and will never belittle or abuse another person by word or action. Such non-violence has the potential to heal the ills of our society.[2]

A profound respect for the person undergirds all faithful relationships, regardless of race, color, creed, social status, physical condition or mental ability. Such regard finds its basis in our being begotten by God through baptism (1 Jn 4:7). Each person has an intimate relationship with God; that is, each one of us is a child of God. That distinction ranks above prestige. Jesus made the quality of our attitude toward others the measure of our love for him: "Whatsoever you do to the least of these, you do to me" (Mt 25:40).

We live in a culture in which this Christian manner of relating to people with respect and love is often superseded by other values. The Western emphasis on productivity has led to society's valuing persons according to accomplishments or prestige rather than their inherent dignity as persons. Consequently, individuals who are economically poor, psychologically impoverished, handicapped or aged often tend to be treated as "lesser" persons.[3] Jesus, however, assures us of our dignity in his words to his disciples at the last meal in John's gospel:

> I call you friends,
> because I have made known to you
> everything I learned from my Father.
> You did not choose me,
> no, I chose you (Jn 15:15–16).

Fidelity to Self

Relationship with self is often a neglected area of attention. The Shakespearian injunction, "To thine own self be true," has perhaps become a cliche uttered with little thought. Nevertheless, this maxim holds volumes of wisdom. To be faithful to ourselves is to know who we are and to live accordingly.

Each one of us is an important person, so much so
that Jesus died in his effort to show us how much God
loves and values each of us. We are children of this great
and loving God, scripture tells us (Gal 3:26), made to God's
own image and likeness (Gen 1:26). Our destiny is to be in
intimate relationship with God forever. That is why God
gave us, Jesus, the Son—that we "may have eternal life" (Jn
3:16). Do we need any other basis for prestige than that?

If we never take time for silence, we lose a sense of
the mystery of our self-worth. We become, as Thomas
Merton wrote, "automaton[s] living without joy...no
longer moved from within, but only from outside."[4] Our
worth is not bound in any way to accomplishments,
intelligence, physical appearance or behavior. Our worth
is rooted solely in God's insatiable love for us, a love
from which no human being is excluded. Being faithful
to ourselves, then, involves accepting God's unconditional love and loving ourselves no less than we love others
(Mt 19:19).

Fidelity to ourselves also involves being patient and
compassionate with ourselves just as the risen Christ is
patient and compassionate with us. But that does not
mean that we will always succeed. Jesus' command to be
perfect as God is perfect (Mt 5:48) is often misinterpreted
as a command to perfection in the English sense of the
word. The Greek word for perfect (*teleios*) does not mean
moral perfection. Rather, it has the sense of a goal of
wholeness to be sought.[5] Therefore, being perfect as God
is perfect in compassion and patience with ourselves
means that we simply strive day after day for wholeness
in our relationships with God and other people.

Fidelity to Family

Of the various types of human relationships, perhaps
marriage is the most vulnerable in our modern society.
Today, there are demands on marriages that our ancestors did not have to face. In years gone by, the patriarchal

pattern of family life prevailed. The husband made the major decisions, the wife helped to execute these decisions, and in turn, she instructed the children to obey them. For the most part, the workplace was limited to men while women maintained the home.

Contemporary society, however, presents a different and challenging agenda for married couples. There is more emphasis on shared decision-making and equality of rights in marriage. Work demands made on both spouses leave them little time to spend with one another. The workplace is shared by women and men alike, often making fidelity an immediate challenge. Because people are living longer, the needs of aging parents also have to be met. When mutual consent in these areas is lacking, the marriage often disintegrates.[6]

Paul's admonitions to husbands and wives in the letter to the Ephesians reflect a society in which women were subject to their husbands. In the household codes of the Roman Empire, the father had authority over the mother, and the mother had authority over the children. The basic attitude that Paul calls for is not one of subjugation, but one of mutual love between husband and wife. Their model for love is that of Christ for the church (Eph 5:22–33). Thus, a faithful marital relationship is one of loving as Christ loves, that is, unconditionally and with a willingness to forgive over and over again. It seeks to express itself in total self-giving love patterned on the love that Christ has for us.

Loyalty to family relationships is more tenuous now than it was in the days of our parents and grandparents. The family meal has almost become a treasured relic of the past. Work schedules, entertainment, sports, and a variety of activities are all rivals for time spent together as family. The high rate of divorce also accounts for much distancing between parents and children, brothers and sisters. Many people today lack the warmth of family support to sustain them during such difficulties as sickness, death and loss of job security.

In spite of the obstacles involved, it is possible for healthy family relationships to develop and be maintained. Moments of faith-sharing have brought many families closer together. Looking at painful family issues such as divorce, alcoholism, or drugs, together in light of the gospel can strengthen and unite a family in times of crisis. A simple sharing about the meaning of the Sunday gospel, or a family's participation in a parish renewal program, has the potential to stimulate growth in faithfulness to one another. Painful experiences shared in faith often find their resurrection in closer family ties and mutual support. Keeping in mind that we are created in God's image helps us to image God's love to one another. It challenges us to be faithful as God is faithful in love, acceptance and forgiveness.

Fidelity to Friends

Friendship finds a perfect paradigm in Jesus' friendship with his disciples, as illustrated earlier in this chapter. In the Old Testament story of David and Jonathan (1 Sam 18–20), we also have another good model. The two men became friends after David defeated Goliath, and his achievement surpassed that of Saul's son, Jonathan. Even though Saul became jealous of David, Jonathan rejoiced in his accomplishments and even defended David from his father's jealous attempts to kill him. A deep and lasting friendship developed between David and Jonathan. In spite of the wickedness of Saul, who repeatedly tried to kill David, David remained faithful to both Jonathan and his father. As Alfred McBride observes, "One of the wonders of friendship is that it covers the multitude of sins not only of the friend, but also of those near and dear to one's friend."[7]

True friendship invites vulnerability; with a good friend, a person can be oneself. Pretensions do not exist between close friends. This trust of one another is very sacred, and if a friendship should break down because of

unfortunate circumstances, it would be morally irrespon-
sible to betray the trust of earlier days in the relationship.
People who have experienced abandonment or betrayal
are often reluctant to trust again. But regardless of the
possible breakdown of friendship, the value and beauty
of true friendship is worth the pain that it may involve.

Relationships between friends are more difficult to
maintain today than in the past. The mobility of our
modern age, frequently made necessary by change of
occupation and just as frequently by choice, puts a strain
on lifelong friendships. Whereas our grandparents were
able to speak of their next door neighbors or their co-
workers as lifelong friends, our experience today is that
our next door neighbors and co-workers sometimes
change as frequently as the seasons. Lack of time and the
cost of keeping contact with distant friends often
account for a weakening of friendship ties. Because of
crime, there is also more reluctance now than in the past
to reach out to strangers who move into a neighborhood.

Human relationships often break down because of
some infidelity on the part of one of the persons
involved. Alfred McBride describes a Christian's attitude
toward wounded love based on that of God as shown us
by Jesus:

> The only cure for betrayal is the love given by
> the one betrayed. The only healing for the hurt
> that is inflicted by the unfaithful one must
> emerge from the balm of forgiveness stored in
> the heart of the innocent partner. Loving fideli-
> ty is the healing response to thoughtless infi-
> delity. Loving forgiveness is the cure for
> heartless rejection.[8]

In spite of the many obstacles to friendship, fidelity is
possible. As children of God, we share God's strength to
be faithful in our love for others and forgiving of their
failures. Even though as human beings we will never

measure up to the fidelity of God, we need an ideal on which to base our relationships.

Fidelity to Co-Workers

As Christians, we have the opportunity to bring the fidelity of Christ to the workplace. By our own faithfulness to Christ-like principles and uprightness, we make God's reign obvious among those with whom we work. When fidelity becomes difficult, the words of Jesus can bring comfort:

> Come to me, all you that are weary and are carrying heavy burdens, and I will give you rest. Take my yoke upon you, and learn from me; for I am gentle and humble in heart, and you will find rest for your souls. For my yoke is easy, and my burden is light (Mt 11:28–30).

Sometimes labor itself seems to lose its sacred character when unfaithfulness pervades the workplace. The scandal of infidelity by government authorities, bank officials, religious leaders and workers of all types has made smaller offenses appear less important to some individuals than before. There is an attitude among many people that, "If our leaders can do it and get by with it, so can we." Others echo a lament similar to that of the prophet Micah over the infidelity of God's people:

> The faithful have disappeared from
> the land,
> and there is no one left who is upright;
> They all lie in wait for blood,
> and they hunt each other with nets... (Mic 7:2).

Micah sums up what is required of every person in order to be faithful to God:

What does God require of you
but to do justice, and to love kindness,
and to walk humbly with your God (Mic 6:8).

Fidelity to co-workers is an area for Christian concern. If each person does his or her fair share of work, then the common good of all is accomplished. Because of its immediate effects on co-workers as well as its long-range and pervasive effects, infidelity in the workplace is a form of oppression. If one person takes the liberty to waste time, the work load for the rest of the employees is increased, and therefore unfair. Infidelity to co-workers reaches far beyond the place of work to the marketplace. Faulty products are frequently the consequence of haphazard labor which in turn causes sickness and even death. One is reminded of the proverb:

Whoever is idle at work
is close kin to a vandal (Prov 18:9; RSV).

Not only are we co-workers with people in the workplace, we are also "God's co-workers" (1 Cor 3:9), St. Paul reminds us. Our work as Christians, then, is done in companionship with God and is part of the creative work of God. The psalmist reminds us of the futility of human toil without God:

If Yahweh does not build the house, in vain do
the builders toil (Ps 127:1; RSV).

If we embrace our role as co-workers with God, it is possible to bring about a transformation of the work environment. The work that we perform becomes work shaped by faith. Our relationships to other people who work with us are then governed by the teachings of Jesus. Much of the drudgery of work dissipates, because we no longer work alone. Our co-worker is the same God who lovingly assures us in the Old Testament, "I have called

you by name. You are mine" (Is 43:1–2; RSV). Having
been made in God's image and likeness, our work is
always to be done in that image and likeness. After each
work that God completed in Genesis 1, the narrative says
that God saw that it was good. Fidelity to God's image
enables us to look at our work and see that it is good.
Then the quality of our work is enhanced as well as our
relationship to co-workers.

Fidelity to Country

Authentic patriotism, or fidelity to one's country,
focuses on the well-being of the whole nation as well as
the world of nations of which it is a part. Christian patriotism manifests itself in love and conveys God's view of
peace, justice and mercy to civic leaders.

Christians who love their country and are devoted to
its progress and well-being support their leaders when
their leadership reflects the values of the gospel. When
that is not the case, they are willing to take the initiative
to bring about change to insure the good of all people. In
this way, Christians who are truly patriotic bring hope to
situations where powerless people have no hope. They
are convinced that with the power of the Spirit received
at baptism, nothing is impossible with God.

Fidelity to one's country is demonstrated by a love
so sincere that a person rejoices in the justice and mercy
shown by one's country but cries out against its sins. The
prophets were aware that injustice to the people, especially the poor and the defenseless, resulted in a weakening of the nation as a whole. They spoke God's word of
criticism, and as a consequence they were often pun-
ished for infidelity to their king. Jeremiah, for example,
was thrown into a cistern for speaking about the future
fall of Jerusalem:

Then the officials said to the king, "This man
ought to be put to death, because he is discour-

aging the soldiers who are left in this city, and
all the people, by speaking such words to
them"....So they took Jeremiah and threw him
into the cistern...letting Jeremiah down by
ropes. Now there was no water in the cistern,
but only mud, and Jeremiah sank in the mud
(Jer 38:4-6).

Jeremiah simply articulated the reality of his country, a
reality that the leaders did not want to hear. He offended
his contemporaries, but he chose to offend human
beings rather than his God who abhorred injustice.

Just as the prophet's word comes to transform the
hearts of people, to bring them to an awareness of their
guilt so, too, does the committed Christian seek to bring
people's hearts and actions to the way of God.

Our own nation came into being as a consequence of
patriotic scrutiny and questioning. Each July our country
recalls with admiration those early colonists who dared
to speak against the injustices heaped upon the people
by their rulers. Throughout our history, patriotic people
have called our nation to accountability for its actions.
Robert McAfee Brown maintains that the only healthy
country is one wherein questioning is not only tolerated
but actually and positively encouraged.[9]

Summary

In spite of the many obstacles, fidelity is possible.
God, who is consistently faithful in loving us regardless of
whether we return that love, is always faithful in forgiving our failures to reciprocate love. Even though as
human beings we will never measure up to the fidelity of
God, we need an ideal on which to base our relationships.

Symbols of fidelity surround us in nature and serve
as reminders of God's constant fidelity to us. Nevertheless,
life in American culture is beset by signs of infidelity in
relationships to God, spouse, friends, co-workers and even

to self. Committed Christians, by their baptismal vows, are called by Christ to imitate the fidelity of the God in whose image they were created. In Jesus, God demonstrated fidelity to the promise God made through the prophet Jeremiah:

> This is the covenant that I will make with the House of Israel after these days, says Yahweh: I will put my laws in their minds, and write them upon their hearts (Jer 31:33; RSV).

Jesus was faithful to God in spite of the difficulties and sufferings that beset him because of his faithfulness. By his fidelity, he established a new covenant between us and God: "Remember, I am with you always, to the end of time" (Mt 28:20). In baptism, his love was poured into our hearts through the Holy Spirit (Rom 5:5). For that reason, fidelity is possible since "God is love, and those who abide in love abide in God, and God abides in them" (1 Jn 4:16). Nevertheless, "if we are unfaithful, God will remain faithful" (2 Tim 2:13).

For Further Reflection:

Ps 23
Ps 34
Ps 103
Lk 15:1–32
Heb 6:17

SUGGESTED READINGS

Alfaro, Juan I. *Justice and Loyalty. A Commentary on the Book of Micah.* Eerdmans, 1989.

Bleske, Elisabeth. "Failure in the Lifelong Project of Fidelity," in *Coping with Failure. Concilium* (1990, No 5), Norbert Greinacher and Norbert Mette, eds. Trinity Press International, 1990, 105–116.

Brown, Robert McAfee. "Patriotic Protest," *Christianity and Crisis* 50 (July 2, 1990) 212–214.

Brueggemann, Walter. *The Prophetic Imagination.* Fortress, 1978.

Graffy, Adrian. *A Prophet Confronts His People.* Biblical Institute Press, 1984.

McBride, Alfred. *Staying Faithful to God, Ourselves, One Another.* St. Anthony Messenger, 1981.

Sakenfeld, K. D. *Faithfulness in Action. Loyalty in Biblical Perspective.* Fortress, 1985.

Notes

1. Harmony with Nature

[1] Quoted from Charles Cummings, *Eco-Spirituality. Toward a Reverent Life* (Paulist, 1991) 50–151.

[2] Glory Pleasants, "Greening Takes Root," *Ambassador* (April, 1991) 54–59.

[3] Thomas A. Sancton, "What On Earth Are We Doing?" *Time* (Jan 2, 1989) 9–10.

[4] Bruce Vawter, *On Genesis* (Doubleday, 1977) 40.

[5] Elizabeth Briere, "Creation, Incarnation and Transfiguration," *Sobernost* 11–12 (1989-1990) 36.

[6] Aldous Huxley as quoted in *The Dorothy Day Book. A Selection from Her Writings and Readings*, eds. Margaret Quigley and Michael Garvey (Templegate, 1982).

[7] Alan B. Durning, "Mobilizing at the Grassroots," *State of the World*, 1989, 173.

2. Citizen and Sojourner

[1] Abraham J. Heschel, *The Prophets* (Harper and Row, 1962) 24.

[2] Heschel, *The Prophets* 5; 25.

[3] R. David Kaylor, *Paul's Covenant Community: Jew and Gentile in Romans* (John Knox 1988) 204–207.

[4] Melanie A. May and Lauree Hersch Mayer, "Citizenship: A Radical Christian Understanding from a Church of the Brethren Perspective," *Midstream* 30 (Oct., 1992) 323–334.

[5] Mary O'Connell, "The Least You Can Do Is Vote," *U.S. Catholic* 52 (May, 1987) 14.

[6] Thomas Jefferson to Edward Carrington, as quoted by

160

Arthur T. Hadley, *The Empty Polling Booth* (Prentice-Hall, 1978) 13.

[7] The United States Catholic Conference, "Political Responsibility: Choices for the Future," *Origins* 17:21 (November 5, 1987) 371.

3. Bridging the Abyss

[1] Walter J. Brueggemann, "The Practice of Homelessness," *Journal for Preachers* 15:4 (1992) 10.

[2] Leo Laberge, "Micah," *The New Jerome Biblical Commentary.* Eds. Raymond E. Brown, Joseph A. Fitzmyer and Roland E. Murphy (Prentice-Hall, 1990) I.251.

[3] Robert Karris, "The Gospel of Luke," *The New Jerome Biblical Commentary.* II.701.

[4] Quoted in *The Dorothy Day Book* Eds. Margaret Quigley and Michael Garvey (Templegate, 1982) 13.

[5] Tony Philpot, "A Home for the Homeless," *Tablet* 246 (Aug. 22, 1992) 1042–43.

[6] *Ibid.*

[7] Alex Vuyst, "Self-Help for the Homeless," *The Humanist* 49 (May/June, 1989) 13.

[8] Dennis Hevesi, *The New York Times* (Saturday, March 16, 1991) L 27.

[9] Ruth Ellen Wasem, *Congressional Research Service Report for Congress, Homelessness and the Federal Response*, 1987–1991.

[10] Bishop Francis Quinn, "Social Needs in a Diocese of Diversity," *Origins* 16 (February 26, 1987) 84–85.

[11] Sharon R. Curtin, *Nobody Ever Died of Old Age* (Little, Brown & Co., 1972) 88.

[12] Curtin, 90.

[13] Jonathan Kozol, *Rachel & Her Children: Homeless Families in America* (Fawcett, 1988).

[14] Stephanie Hollyman and Victoria Irwin, *We the Homeless* (Philosophical Library, Inc., 1988) 11.

[15] J. Brian Hehir, "Homelessness Today—and Tomorrow," *Origins* 16 (February 26, 1987) 656.

[16] "The Right to a Decent Home: A Pastoral Response to the Crisis in Housing," U.S. Catholic Conference, Washington, D.C., 1975, No. 8.

[17] "The Right to a Decent Home," No. 9.

[18] "The Right to a Decent Home," No. 101.

[19] Bishop Francis Quinn, "Social Needs in a Diocese of Diversity," 85.

[20] For other suggestions, see "20 Ways You Can Help the Homeless," *St. Anthony Messenger* (March, 1992) 21.

[21] Bishop Francis Quinn, "Social Needs in a Diocese of Diversity," 84.

4. Encountering the Alien

[1] Donald E. Gowan, "Wealth and Poverty in the Old Testament: The Case of the Widows, the Orphan, and the Sojourner," *Interpretation* 41 (1987) 341–353.

[2] Claus Westermann, *Genesis 12-36*. Trans. by John Scullion (Augsburg, 1985) 276–277.

[3] Patrick D. Miller, Jr., "Israel as Host to Strangers," *Today's Immigrants and Refugees* (NCCB, 1988) 1–19.

[4] Miller, 1–9.

[5] Helen Koenig Mainelli, "Aliens in Our Midst," *The Bible Today* (July, 1991) 206–207.

[6] Roland de Vaux, *Ancient Israel.* 2 volumes (McGraw-Hill, 1965) I.74–76.

[7] Joseph Blenkinsopp, "Deuteronomy," *The New Jerome Biblical Commentary.* Eds. Raymond E. Brown, Joseph A. Fitzmyer and Roland E. Murphy (Prentice-Hall, 1990) I.105.

[8] See Lawrence Boadt, *Reading the Old Testament* (Paulist, 1984) 120–121.

[9] W. H. Bellinger, Jr., *Psalms. Reading and Studying the Book of Praises* (Hendrickson, 1990) 6.

[10] J. H. Elliott, *A Home for the Homeless* (Fortress: 1981).

[11] David W. Augsburger, *Pastoral Counseling across Cultures* (Westminster, 1986) 55–56.

[12] *Ibid.*

[13] For example, an encyclical on the missions by Pope John XXIII and the Vatican II document, *Ad Gentes.*

[14] Timothy M. Matovina, "Hispanic Catholics in the U.S.: No Melting Pot in Sight," *America* (Mar 16, 1991) 289–290.

5. Embracing the Church Feminine

[1] Raymond E. Brown, *The Community of the Beloved Disciple* (Paulist, 1979) 195–196.

[2] Bruce J. Malina and Jerome H. Neyrey, "First Century Personality," *The Social World of Luke-Acts.* Ed. Jerome H. Neyrey (Hendrickson, 1991) 86.

[3] Joseph A. Grassi, *The Secret Identity of the Beloved Disciple* (Paulist, 1992) 74.

[4] Luke Timothy Johnson, "Luke 24:1–11," *Interpretation* 46:1 (Jan. 1992) 57.

[5] Joachim Jeremias, *Jerusalem in the Time of Jesus* (Fortress, 1969) 376.

[6] Joseph A. Fitzmyer, "The Letter to the Romans," The New Jerome Biblical Commentary. Eds. Raymond E. Brown et al. (Prentice-Hall, 1990) II.867. Fitzmyer points out that there is no certain evidence that "deacon" or "deaconess" was already a designation for a special group of ministers in the church at that early period. For an opposite view, see Elisabeth Schussler Fiorenza, *In Memory of Her. A Feminist Theological Reconstruction of Christian Origins* (Crossroad, 1983) 47–48.

[7] Joseph Fitzmyer, "The Letter to the Romans," II.868.

[8] John E. Stambaugh and David Balch, *The New Testament and Its Social Environment* (Westminster, 1986) 142.

[9] For a discussion of the post-Pauline letters, see Raymond E. Brown, *The Churches the Apostles Left Behind* (Paulist, 1984) 13–60.

[10] See, for example, Raymond E. Brown, *The Churches the Apostles Left Behind*, 43–44.

[11] D. C. Verner, *The Household of God: The Social World of the Pastoral Epistles* (Scholars Press, 1983).

[12] Jerome Murphy-O'Connor, O.P., "The First Letter to the Corinthians," *The New Jerome Biblical Commentary*, eds. R. E. Brown et al. (Prentice-Hall, 1990) II.811.

[13] Paul J. Kobelski, "The Letter to the Ephesians," *The New Jerome Biblical Commentary*, eds. Raymond E. Brown, Joseph A. Fitzmyer and Roland E. Murphy (Prentice-Hall, 1990) II: No. 55, 883–890.

[14] Donald Senior, "Roles of Women in Scripture: A Perspective from the Church's Universal Mission," *Women in the Church* (The Pastoral Press, 1987) 13.

[15] Quoted in *Christifideles Laici* 49. English translation, "The Vocation and the Mission of the Faithful in the Church and in the World," December 30, 1988.

[16] *Christifideles Laici* 49.

[17] David W. Augsburger, *Pastoral Counseling Across Cultures* (Westminster, 1986) 223.

[18] Donald Senior, "Roles of Women in Scripture," 4–5.

[19] *Lumen Gentium*, 32. Also see Sister Sharon Euart, "Women and the 1983 Code of Canon Law," *Origins* 20:28 (December 20, 1990) 453, an address to the National Conference of Catholic Bishops' Committee on Women in Society and in the Church.

6. Growing Older

[1] Miriam Corcoran, S.C.N., *In Ourselves Growing Older.* Eds. Paula Doress and Diana Siegel (Simon & Schuster, 1987).

[2] John Gillman, "Going Home to the Lord," *The Bible Today* (September, 1982) 275–281.

[3] Sharon Curtin, *Nobody Ever Died of Old Age* (Little, Brown and Company, 1972) 227.

[4] S. H. Blank, "Old Age," *IDB.2* (Abingdon,1962) 55.

[5] D. B. Bromley, *The Psychology of Human Aging* (Pelican Books, 1974) 312.

[6] John S. Kselman and Michael L. Barre, "Psalms," *The New Jerome Biblical Commentary.* Eds. Raymond E. Brown, Joseph A. Fitzmyer, Roland E. Murphy (Prentice-Hall, 1990) I.538.87.

[7] Julie Sly, "Why We Need a Spirituality of Aging," *St. Anthony Messenger* 99 (June, 1991) 18.

[8] *Ibid.,* 19.

[9] *Ibid.*

[10] Bill Kelly, "Scripture Sharing with Seniors," *Liguorian* 77 (Apr., 1989) 24–25.

166 GIFT AND RESPONSE

[11] Sly, 20.

[12] D. B. Bromley, *The Psychology of Human Aging*, 377.

[13] Margaret Hellie Huyck, *Growing Older* (Prentice-Hall, 1974) 133.

7. Keeping Fit for Life in Christ

[1] John A. T. Robinson, *The Body* (SCM Press, 1966) 9.

[2] Joseph A. Fitzmyer, "Pauline Theology," *The New Jerome Biblical Commentary*. Eds. Raymond E. Brown, Joseph A. Fitzmyer and Roland E. Murphy (Prentice-Hall, 1990) II.82:102.

[3] Fitzmyer, "Pauline Theology," II.82:122.

[4] Fitzmyer, "The Letter to the Romans," *The Jerome Biblical Commentary*. II.51:113.

[5] Elizabeth Briere, "Creation, Incarnation and Transfiguration," *Sobernost* 11-12 (1989-1990) 38.

[6] Briere, "Creation, Incarnation and Transfiguration," 31-40.

[7] Alvyn Petterson, "Athanasius' Presentation of Antony of the Desert's Admiration for His Body" in *Studia Patristica* XXI. Ed. E. A. Livingstone (Peeters Press, 1989) 438-447.

[8] Thomas Merton, *Contemplation in a World of Action* (Doubleday, 1973) 116-117.

[9] Margaret R. Miles, *Fullness of Life: Historical Foundations for a New Asceticism* (Westminster, 1981) 157-58.

[10] Thomas Merton, *Thomas Merton in Alaska* (New Directions: 1988) 154.

[11] Merton, *Contemplation* 118.

[12] Miles, *Fullness of Life*, 161.

[13] *Ibid.*

[14] Paul Brand and Philip Young, *Fearfully and Wonderfully Made* (Zondervan, 1980).

8. Fidelity in Relationships

[1] Katherine Doob Sakenfeld, *Faithful in Action: Loyalty in Biblical Perspective* (Fortress, 1985) 39; 140–141.

[2] Bernard Häring, *The Healing Power of Peace and Non-Violence* (Paulist, 1986) 66–79.

[3] Gotthard Fuchs, "Does God Fail?" *Coping With Failure.* Edited by Norbert Greinacher and Norbert Mette (Concilium, 1990, No 5) 130.

[4] Thomas Merton, *The Silent Life* (Farrar, Straus & Cudahy, 1970).

[5] Daniel Harrington, *The Gospel of Matthew* (Liturgical Press, 1991) 90.

[6] Elisabeth Bleske, "Failure in the Lifelong Project of Fidelity," *Coping With Failure.* Edited by Norbert Greinacher and Norbert Mette (Concilium, 1990, No. 5) 107-113.

[7] Alfred McBride, *Staying Faithful to God, Ourselves, One Another* (St. Anthony Messenger, 1981) 66.

[8] McBride, 61.

[9] Robert McAfee Brown, "Patriotic Protest," *Christianity and Crisis* 50 (July 2, 1990) 212.